CW00765217

بسم الله الرحمن الرحيم

DEPRESSION & ANXIETY

THE CAUSES & TREATMENT ACCORDING TO THE QUR'ĀN

Based on the Television Series

By
Imam Muḥammad Saʿīd Ramaḍān al-Būṭī

Translated & Summarised by
Mahdi Lock & Hazem Nasr

We at The Foreword Publications and Nawa Books would like to express our appreciation to everybody who contributed to making this book a reality. We pray that Allah ﷻ bestow His blessings upon it by guiding readers of this book closer towards Allah ﷻ and His beloved Prophet Muhammad ﷺ.

Depression and Anxiety: The Causes and Treatment According to the Qurʾān, based on the Television Series الكآبـة .. أسـباب وعـلاج by Imam Muḥammad Saʿīd Ramaḍān Al-Būṭī.

Published by:	Nawa Books & The Foreword Publications
Published in:	July 2023
Presented by:	Imam Muḥammad Saʿīd Ramaḍān Al-Būṭī
Translated & Summarised by:	Mahdi Lock and Hazem Nasr

ISBN:	978-981-18-7636-3
Cover by:	Muhammadan Press

سَهِرَتْ أَعيُنٌ وَنامَت عُيونُ

في أُمورٍ تَكونُ أَو لا تَكونُ

فَادرَأِ الهَمَّ ما استَطَعتَ عَنِ النَفـ

ـسِ فَحِملانُكَ الهُمومَ جُنونُ

إِنَّ رَبّاً كَفاكَ بِالأَمسِ ماكا

نَ سَيَكفيكَ في غَدٍ ما يَكونُ

***

Some eyes stay awake and some sleep,

Regarding matters that could be or not be.

As much as you are able to, keep worry away from the soul;

Weighing yourself down with worries is madness.

Your Lord sufficed you yesterday with what was;

He will suffice you tomorrow with what will be.

(Imam ash-Shāfiʿī ﵀)

Contents

About Imam Muḥammad Saʿīd Ramaḍan al-Būṭī I

About the Authors III

Introduction by Mahdi Lock 1

Chapter 1:
What Are the Underlying Causes of Depression and Anxiety? 5

Chapter 2:
The First Cause: Not Knowing the Reality of Life 17

Chapter 3:
The Second Cause: Fear of the Future 29

Chapter 4:
The Third Cause: Fear of Adversity and Affliction 41

Chapter 5:
The Third Cause (Continued): Fear of Adversity and Affliction - Having No Hope of Forgiveness 57

Chapter 6:
The Fourth Cause: The Fear of Death 71

Chapter 7:
The Fifth Cause: The Inability to Achieve Personal Ambitions 83

Chapter 8: 95
The Fifth Cause: The Inability to Achieve Personal Ambitions (Continued)
Cognitive-Behavioural Therapy: Part One

Chapter 9: 109
The Fifth Cause: The Inability to Achieve Personal Ambitions (Continued)
Cognitive-Behavioural Therapy: Part Two

Chapter 10: 125
Is Sorcery a Cause of Depression?

Appendix A: 135
Causes of Depression and Their Remedies

Appendix B: 141
Man's Love for Allah

Appendix C: 151
How Do You Treat Depression?

Appendix D: 157
Mental Illness

About Imam Muḥammad Saʿīd Ramaḍan al-Būṭī

Imam Muḥammad Saʿīd Ramaḍan Al-Būṭī is one of the foremost Muslim theologians and legal scholars of this age. Born in 1929 in the village of Ayn Dewar in northern Syria, the imam moved to Damascus at the age of four with his father, the great scholar Mullā Ramaḍān al-Būṭī ﵀, where he received his primary and secondary education. In 1953, he joined the Faculty of Sharīʿah at the University of al-Azhar in Cairo, Egypt, graduating with a first class in 1955. The following year he obtained a Diploma in Education from the Faculty of Arabic Language at the same University.

In 1958, the Imam was appointed as a teacher at the secondary school in Homs and in 1961, he was appointed as a lecturer in the Faculty of Sharīʿah at the University of Damascus. In 1965, at the University of al-Azhar once again, he obtained his doctorate with high distinction and a recommendation for a teaching post. That same year, he was appointed as a teacher in the Faculty of Sharīʿah at the University of Damascus, then an assistant professor and finally a full professor. He became the vice dean of that college in 1975 and then the dean in 1977. A few years later, he was appointed head of the department of Theology and Comparative Religion.

In addition to his lecturing, Imam al-Būṭī wrote around sixty books covering various Islamic sciences and subjects, the most prominent ones being *Fiqh al-Sīrah* (The Jurisprudence of the Prophetic Biography), *Kubrā al-Yaqīniyyāt al-Kawniyyah* (The Greatest Universal Sureties) and his four-volume commentary on the spiritual aphorisms of Imam Ibn ʿAṭāʾillāh al-Askandarī. He was also very active in teaching common believers in local masjids, especially Masjid al-Īmān in Damascus, and on television, recordings of which can be found online and especially on the site www.naseemalsham.com. He also served as the imam at the Umayyad Grand Masjid in Damascus for Friday prayers, a post he held for decades.

On March 21, 2013, Imam al-Būtī, along with approximately fifty students, was murdered by terrorists while teaching Qurʾānic commentary in Masjid al-Īmān. Despite the immense trials and tribulations that Syria was and is still enduring, Imam al-Būṭī was never dissuaded from his dedicated service to knowledge. After a funeral prayer that was attended by thousands of people, the Imam was buried next to Imam Ṣalāḥ al-Dīn al-Ayyūbī in Bāb al-Saghīr graveyard in Damascus. May the Lord bless and have mercy on him and all of us.

About the Authors

Mahdi Lock

Mahdi Lock is a professional freelance translator of classical Arabic Islamic texts into English. He has a BA in Arabic and History from the University of Leeds, an MA in Arabic Linguistics from King Abdul Aziz University in Jeddah, and a Diploma in Translation from the Chartered Institute of Linguists in London, of which he is also a Member (MCIL). He has been studying theology, law and other Islamic sciences for several years with teachers in England, North Africa and the Middle East.

To date, his translated works include:

- *Kitāb al-Ḥalāl wa al-Ḥarām* by Imam Abū Ḥāmid al-Ghazālī
- *Kitāb al-Waqf* from *al-Mughnī al-Muḥtāj* by al-Khaṭīb al-Shirbīnī
- The introduction to *al-Majmūʿ* by Imam Yaḥyā al-Nawawī
- *Sharḥ al-Ṣudūr* by Imam Jalāl al-Dīn al-Suyūṭī
- Almost 2000 pages of the *Khawāṭir* of Imam Muḥammad Mutawalli ash-Shaʿrawī (http://www.elsharawyreflections.com/)
- *La Dhukūriyyah fī al-Fiqh* by Imam Muḥammad at-Tāwīl
- *Manhaj al-Ḥaḍārah al-Insāniyyah fī al-Qurʾān* by Imam Muḥammad Saʿīd Ramaḍān al-Būṭī

For Nawa Books, he has translated the following:

- *Al-Wāfī: A Thorough Commentary on the Forty Nawawiyyah* by Imams Muṣṭafā al-Bughā and Muḥyī ad-Dīn Mistū
- *Man and Allah's Justice on Earth, Inward Sin, A Unique Pedagogical Approach in the Qurʾān, To Every Young Woman Who Believes in Allah, Islam and the Problems of the Youth*, all of which are part of the Pinnacle Papers series by Imam Muḥammad Saʿīd Ramaḍān al-Būṭī
- The first volume of *al-Fiqh al-Manhajī ʿalā Madhhab al-Imām ash-Shāfiʿī*, by Imams Muṣṭafā al-Bughā, Alī ash-Sharbajī, and Muṣṭafā al-Khin ﵏
- *The Rights of the Husband and Wife* by Shaykh ʿAbdul Hādī al-Kharsah
- *Remembrances & Etiquettes of The Prophet* ﷺ

Mahdi has also been teaching English and Arabic for about two decades, from primary school through to the university level. He teaches other sciences privately, mainly fiqh, and regularly does online study circles, such as the Halaqah Book Club.

You can follow Mahdi online via his eponymous blog, where he posts translations of fatwas, khutbahs, articles, and other beneficial material, and his YouTube channel (@TheForeword), where he posts podcasts on various topics and translations from the classes and lectures of ʿulamāʾ.

Hazem Nasr Mahdy

Hazem Nasr Mahdy was born in Egypt but has lived in different parts of the world since childhood, including Europe, North America, and both the Middle and Far East. His teen years were spent in Denmark, where he met and attended high school with his long-life friend and co-author of this book, Mahdi Lock. He has a BA in Economics from the American University in Cairo and an MBA from Hong Kong University. He speaks Arabic and English at a native level and accordingly, his journey with translating started by supporting Mahdi Lock in proofreading and editing the works of Imam Muhammad Saʿīd Ramaḍān al-Būṭī, such as *The Approach to Human Civilization in the Qurʾān, Man and Allah's Justice on Earth, To Every Young Woman Who Believes In Allah, A Unique Pedagogical Approach in the Qurʾān*, and *Islam and the Problems of the Youth*. The book in your hands is the first joint effort between the co-authors.

Introduction

All praise belongs to Allah, Lord of all creation, who forgives sins and with Him alone is every success. And may Allah's blessings and peace be upon the Messenger of Allah and all of his Family and Companions, ameen.

Imam al-Būṭī ﷺ says in his introduction to this series,

"In the name of Allah, the All-Merciful, the Most Merciful, Praise be to Allah, Lord of all Creation.

O Allah, remove us from the darkness of illusion and honour us with the light of understanding.

And may the best blessings and peace be upon our master, Muhammad, and upon all his Family and Companions.

We shall discuss, with success from Allah ﷻ a subject that is perhaps of the utmost importance.

How does the Qurʾān treat the illnesses of depression, anxiety, and psychological unrest in human beings?

We will start treating this topic in response to the wishes that have reached us requesting that we urgently address this subject and elucidate the Qurʾān's role in putting an end to this dangerous epidemic, which, today, afflicts many people around the world.

We ask Allah ﷻ for success. And we ask Him ﷻ that we do it properly".

Depression and anxiety are hot topics nowadays and have been for several years. Many people suffer from one of the two, or both, or know someone who does. Indeed, just about everyone feels sad or anxious at one time or another. Such is the nature of this world.

But where do these feelings come from, and how can they be mitigated or even removed?

The book in your hands is based on a television series, Depression - Causes and Treatment[1], presented by Imam Muḥammad Saʿīd Ramaḍān al-Būṭī . It consists of ten 30-minute episodes. However, we have decided to name the book, "Depression & Anxiety - Causes and Treatment", since the Imam frequently mentions anxiety alongside depression. What you are about to read is not directly from the Imam but a translation and summary of his words. Whatever mistakes and errors it contains are our fault and not his.[2]

There are also some important points to bear in mind:

1. While this book is on the topic of depression and anxiety, it should *not* be viewed as a textbook or manual of psychology. Rather, it should be regarded as a book on *iḥsān*, *zuhd*, and *tazkiyyah*, i.e. spiritual enrichment, detaching from the world, and purification of the heart and soul. According to the Oxford English Dictionary (OED), *psychology* originally meant 'the study or consideration of the soul or spirit'; that is now rare. The current, prevalent meaning is 'the scientific study of the nature,

1 الكآبة .. أسباب وعلاج The series is also part of a larger series called دراسات قرآنية, i.e. Qurʾānic Studies. Thus, this series, and the book in your hands, looks at the causes of depression and anxiety and how they can be treated according to the Qurʾān.

2 This also means that we have removed or edited any first-person references or mentions of the imam's personal experiences. Furthermore, where the imam makes mention of certain statistics or phenomena, we have added sources. And with Allah alone is every success.

functioning, and development of the human mind'.[3] Thus, this book can only be considered a book of psychology according to the earlier definition, and that is in the sense that these problems, namely depression and anxiety, stem from the spirit, and are not confined to the mind.[4]

2. What the reader will find is that Imam al-Būṭī is talking about certain types of depression and anxiety and linking them to certain causes. For example, there is a type of depression and anxiety that is caused by a fear of growing old and dying. There is another type that is caused by a fear of affliction and adversity, and yet another caused by the inability to fulfil one's ambitions. And so forth.

3. The imam calls these causes "hidden" or "underlying"; they are causes that most people might not consider or even think about, especially within a secular paradigm.

4. This means that the cure or treatment for these types of depression and anxiety ultimately rests in one's relationship with Allah ﷻ. This should not be controversial at all. There is *always* room for improvement in your relationship with Allah. To believe that you are 'just fine' is a spiritual malady in and of itself, which is that of self-satisfaction, which is connected to pride. A Muslim should always welcome the invitation to draw nearer to Allah, to draw nearer to his Lord truthfully and sincerely. Furthermore, knowing that drawing nearer to Allah is where the cure lies is immensely empowering; it means that you have control. You can do something about your life. Instead of seeing it as your fault or burden, see it as your responsibility

3 https://www.oed.com/view/Entry/153907?redirectedFrom=psychology#eid (Accessed 29 December, 2022).

4 See Appendix D: Mental Illness.

and that you only have this responsibility because you are capable of doing something. You are not helpless when you have Allah's help.[5]

5. Learning about depression and anxiety and understanding them, i.e. by drawing nearer to Allah and understanding why one was created, is not going to make one's calamities and trials go away. Rather, it should make one competent and strong enough to deal with them, such that they do not make one feel anxious or depressed.

6. Appendices have been added to add further clarity on the topic, and to provide the reader with additional resources with which he can increase his knowledge and understanding.

And with Allah alone is every success.

5 The book *Inward Sin* by Imam al-Būṭī is one of the best resources on this topic, and Allah knows best.

Chapter One

What Are the Underlying Causes of Depression and Anxiety?

To start, it is necessary to ask about the underlying causes behind this illness that attacks many souls in this age, whether in developed or developing nations.

The first question is:

What are the underlying factors behind what is called "depression", as well as "anxiety" or "psychological unrest", which holds sway over so many people?

These underlying factors can be narrowed down to five main causes, which will be covered in the following order:

1) Not Knowing the Reality of Life

The first cause is the most important one and its victims are many.

This first cause is embodied in the ignorance of life's secrets, what comes after it (i.e, the Hereafter), the purpose of man's existence and then his departure from this existence.

This first cause haunts the many people who are ignorant of the reality of this life. They have opened their eyes to this life but without having received convincing knowledge about its reality, its secrets, the Hereafter, and the reason why man comes into this world for some time and then leaves.

So, why does he come into this world, and why does he leave?

What is life and what are its secrets?

These questions trouble many people, as they have not had the opportunity to learn their answers from their proper, scientific source, from the Creator of life, from the One who has created this existence and created this universe that we live in.

As you know, this ignorance and the insistence on finding the answers to this mysterious issue drives man into a serious and dangerous state of anxiety and unrest. And you might be aware that this anxiety and unrest were translated at one point in time into a philosophy (Existentialism).

What is existentialist philosophy based on and what are its pillars?

The pillars of this philosophy are psychological, not intellectual. These psychological pillars are related to the anxiety and distress that surrounded man after each of the two world wars. This anxiety and distress are embodied in the words of the leading existentialists, who claim that this life quashes man with failure, anxiety, and despair.

That is the destiny of man (according to them). He aspires to great and important things but his limited abilities fail him. He aspires to remain in the bliss which he enjoys but he inevitably reaches a ceiling. He dreams and imagines himself gaining great opportunities in his life, but again, his abilities prevent him from reaching them.

This situation makes man ruminate failure, which often elicits fear and feelings of hopelessness. Existentialist philosophy stemmed from these three issues. Many people have gone mad because of the distress and anxiety resulting from the ignorance of life, its secrets, and why man comes into this life for a short time and then leaves.

2) Fear of the Future

The second cause is the fear of what the unknown future might bring. There are many people who are described as being highly sensitive. This delicate over-sensitivity drives them to look for the future that awaits them.

What will become of them tomorrow?

If this person is in his youth, how will he spend his youth? And what will his life be like?

He does not know.

If his youth abandons him and the vigour that accompanies youth is no longer what it was and he becomes elderly, what will be his condition then?

How will he abandon the desires and passions that he is currently enjoying and is accustomed to?

For people who are described as being highly sensitive, these questions and wondering what the future will bring drive many of them into psychological unrest and anxiety.

3) Fear of Adversity and Affliction

The third cause is the constraint and pressure that some people might face because of the adversities of life and the causes of misery and pain; bodily pain such as disease as well as psychological pain.

Some people see others around them, such as neighbours or friends, enjoying wealth whereas their own "bad luck", as they would call it, willed them to be poor. They have tried and strived (to be affluent), but their efforts have come to no avail. Everyone around them is blessed with health and wellbeing, which is visible on their glowing faces and in their appearance, while their bad luck, once again, has struck them with different maladies afflicting their bodies.

They become a focal point for different diseases and when they see those around them who were spared from disease, this further adds to their own pain and feelings of constraint and pressure. Similarly, they look at the different tragedies afflicting their families, or the accidents, calamities, and things of that nature that distress them.

Of course, anyone's life is prone to such things. These things afflict some people more than others. People vary in these matters.

However, they view themselves as people who are confounded with bad luck and faced with a reality that contradicts what they had hoped for, whether in the case of the good health that they hoped for, wealth and riches, a happy and healthy family, their safety and tranquillity, or anything else that was absent from their lives.

When these people place so much value on this life being the one and only chance for success and happiness, this matter becomes one of the most serious causes behind the outbreak of anxiety and distress in their souls.

4) The Fear Of Death

The fourth cause is the fear of death, which is certainly the end of every life form. When this fear gets a hold of certain people, they become obsessed with the phenomenon of death, its effects and its manifestations, such as the funeral, the burial, and then ending up in a grave. This causes them to compare their current reality (i.e. above the ground) with what awaits them underground amidst the dust.

There are many people who constantly reflect on death, talk about it, and visualise it. As a result, an obsession grabs hold of their thoughts and imaginations. This obsession that haunts them also drives them into a state of anxiety and psychological unrest.

5) The Inability To Achieve Personal Ambitions

The fifth cause is the inability to achieve the personal hopes and ambitions that one is striving towards.

For example, a person was hoping to become a prominent businessman, or aspiring to obtain a distinguished academic degree in a certain field. In many cases, the reality that this person is faced with distances him and separates him from his goal, and this is often a source of stress and unrest that keeps growing, and eventually drives him towards more serious psychological conditions, such as anxiety.

These are the different causes that result in the phenomenon of depression, anxiety or what is referred to as "psychological unrest".[6] Whether you go to developed nations or developing nations, you will find that these are the five main causes.

6 Individuals with an anxiety disorder often meet criteria for a depressive disorder or other psychological disorder. See 'Correlates of Quality of Life in Anxiety Disorders: Review of Recent Research': https://doi.org/10.1007/s11920-021-01290-4 (Accessed 29 November, 2022).

Those who live in developed or secular societies tend to suffer more from depression and anxiety than those who live in developing or Islamic societies.

You will discover the reason behind this when the core of the subject is delved into and analysed, and the role of the Qurʾān in protecting people from these dangerous illnesses and ailments is clarified.

Of course, you also know that the poor and those that live in developing countries are not exempt from these illnesses and ailments. However, those who live under the bright lights of the city tend to suffer much more than those that live in less developed countries today. Furthermore, those who are Muslim merely because of tradition and custom are also not exempt from these illnesses and ailments. All of this will be made clear later.

Now, let us turn to the Book of Allah ﷻ (i.e. the Qurʾān).

Does the Book of Allah ﷻ play an effective role in protecting people from these illnesses?

Yes, but before everything else, consider the Qurʾānic verses in which the Qurʾān promises to protect the people that interact with it, believe in it, and implement its prescriptions, and how the Qurʾān promises to place them in a safe haven from these illnesses.

First, listen to these promises that the Qurʾān has made and, after that, one can ask:

How does the Qurʾān implement these promises?

How does the Qurʾān introduce to people, and the different groups they belong to, the remedies that protect them from the consequences of these causes that have just been listed?

First, look at this promise in the Book Of Allah ﷻ. He ﷻ says:

﴿يَٰٓأَيُّهَا ٱلنَّاسُ قَدۡ جَآءَتۡكُم مَّوۡعِظَةٞ مِّن رَّبِّكُمۡ وَشِفَآءٞ لِّمَا فِي ٱلصُّدُورِ﴾

"Mankind! Admonition has come to you from your Lord and also healing for what is in the heart" [Yūnus 10:57]

"Mankind! Admonition has come to you" in the Qurʾān "from your Lord and also healing for what is in the heart". Notice the words "healing for what is in the heart".

Where is anxiety found?

Inside the heart.

Unrest is also in the heart.

Allah ﷻ is telling us that a remedy has come to us from our Lord to protect our hearts from anxiety and to cure them from all the reasons that lead to anxiety and unrest.

That is a promise.

Some of you might ask: where is the credibility of this promise?

This shall be answered later.

Here is another promise, a confirmation of the first promise. Allah ﷻ is addressing all of humanity but in the form of addressing their parents, Adam and Ḥawwāʾ[7]:

﴿قَالَ ٱهۡبِطَا مِنۡهَا جَمِيعَۢاۖ بَعۡضُكُمۡ لِبَعۡضٍ عَدُوّٞۖ فَإِمَّا يَأۡتِيَنَّكُم
مِّنِّي هُدٗى فَمَنِ ٱتَّبَعَ هُدَايَ فَلَا يَضِلُّ وَلَا يَشۡقَىٰ ١٢٣ وَمَنۡ أَعۡرَضَ

7 i.e. Eve.

عَـن ذِكْـرِى فَـإِنَّ لَـهُۥ مَعِيشَـةً ضَنـكًا﴾

"He said, 'Go down from it, all of you, as enemies to one another! But when guidance comes to you from Me, all those who follow My guidance will not go astray and will not be miserable. But if anyone turns away from My reminder, his life will be a dark and narrow one'"
[Ṭaha 20:123-124]

Allah said: "Go down from it". Allah ﷻ ordained that Adam, Ḥawwāʿ, and their descendants until the Day of Judgement reside on this Earth "as enemies to one another" for a wisdom that shall be explained later.

However, who are the ones that are rescued from this reality?

They are those who listen to Allah's ﷻ instructions and implement them. Allah ﷻ says:

"But when guidance comes to you from Me, all those who follow My guidance will not go astray and will not be miserable." They will not suffer from the causes that lead to anxiety or psychological unrest.

Then Allah ﷻ discusses the opposite case; whoever rejects My remembrance and the instructions that will come to you, "his life will be a dark and narrow one". They will lead a constrained life. They will feel stifled whether they live in a state of abundance and affluence or in a state of poverty, or whether they enjoy good health or suffer from multiple diseases: "his life will be a dark and narrow one".

Another divine promise is confirmed by Allah's ﷻ statement:

﴿مَنْ عَمِلَ صَٰلِحًا مِّن ذَكَرٍ أَوْ أُنثَىٰ وَهُوَ مُؤْمِنٌ فَلَنُحْيِيَنَّهُۥ حَيَوٰةً
طَيِّبَةً ۖ وَلَنَجْزِيَنَّهُمْ أَجْرَهُم بِأَحْسَنِ مَا كَانُوا۟ يَعْمَلُونَ﴾

"Anyone who acts rightly, male or female, being a believer, We will give them a good life and We will recompense them according to the best of what they did."
[An-Naḥl 16:97]

This means that whoever acts rightly while he is a believer, that is, those who listen to My instructions and implement them, "We will give them a good life".

Pause at this promise that Allah ﷻ has committed Himself to. Allah ﷻ has promised to make these people lead a good and fortunate life.

What is a good life?

It is when the heart is far from anxiety, unrest, and their causes, and it feels safe and secure. That is the good life, regardless of appearances, because if one enjoys a good life where pleasure flutters in the heart, it does not matter if one lives in a small house or a large palace. It is all the same to him. If security and joy flutter within the heart, then what does it matter whether his wealth is abundant and plentiful or scarce and limited. It makes no difference. The inner self is what is important, not the outward appearance.

Is there anywhere else where Allah reiterates this promise?

Indeed, look at Allah's ﷻ statement:

﴿ٱلَّذِينَ ءَامَنُوا۟ وَلَمْ يَلْبِسُوٓا۟ إِيمَٰنَهُم بِظُلْمٍ أُو۟لَٰٓئِكَ لَهُمُ
ٱلْأَمْنُ وَهُم مُّهْتَدُونَ﴾

"Those who have faith[8] and do not mix up their faith with any wrongdoing, they are the ones who are safe[9]; it is they who are guided." [al-Anʿām 6:82]

The wording "mix up their faith with any wrongdoing" is very precise. This means those who do not use faith for their own benefit and whims, "they are the ones who are safe; it is they who are guided".

The word "safe" includes so many different meanings and contains so many factors that lead to man's happiness. Safety is something that is extremely valuable in the life of a human being. Money on its own cannot achieve safety, nor can knowledge alone bring safety into existence. Civilization, in its purely material form (i.e. not backed up by knowledge and etiquette), cannot achieve safety either.

The only one who can create safety is the One who created the heart ﷻ.

Where does safety reside?

In the heart.

And who created the heart?

Allah the Exalted, who created both man and his heart.

Only this Lord that created the heart can insert what He ﷻ calls "safety" into the heart.

If safety is spread throughout the heart, the means of happiness have been achieved.

---

8 Ar. *al-īmān*.

9 Ar. *al-amn*.

Who does Allah ﷻ promise safety and security?

"Those who have faith and do not mix up their faith with any wrongdoing".

Those who give their faith its right in how they conduct themselves and do not exploit their faith and deeds for the benefit of their worldly affairs. This would be a form of deception with Allah ﷻ. However, Allah ﷻ promises those who do not exploit their faith that He will bless them with security.

Has Allah ﷻ made any more promises to keep His slaves away from anxiety and psychological unrest?

He certainly has, including His statement:

﴿ٱللَّهُ وَلِيُّ ٱلَّذِينَ ءَامَنُواْ يُخْرِجُهُم مِّنَ ٱلظُّلُمَٰتِ إِلَى ٱلنُّورِ ۖ وَٱلَّذِينَ كَفَرُوٓاْ أَوْلِيَآؤُهُمُ ٱلطَّٰغُوتُ يُخْرِجُونَهُم مِّنَ ٱلنُّورِ إِلَى ٱلظُّلُمَٰتِ﴾

"Allah is the Protector of those who have faith. He brings them out of the darkness into the light. While the disbelievers have false gods as protectors. They take them from the light into the darkness." [al-Baqarah 2:257]

Have you once again noticed these precise words?

"Allah is the Protector of those who have faith", i.e. those who have implemented their faith, enlivened it through deeds and behaviour, and implemented the instructions of Allah ﷻ. Allah ﷻ is the ally and protector of those people. And by the virtue of Allah's support and care for them, He must remove them from the darkness of misery, psychological unrest, anxiety, and all these causes that have been discussed, to the light of hope, tranquillity, stability, and contentment. Indeed, Allah ﷻ will inevitably honour these people with the fruits of what they did.

Then Allah ﷻ compares these people to their opposites. He said:

"while the disbelievers have false gods as protectors", which means Shayṭān and his accomplices among mankind. They take man out of the light and into darkness. They remove him from the landscape of security and into the darkness of anxiety, unrest, and psychological misery. You might find a person who is surrounded by glamorous bliss but the darkness of anxiety dominates his heart.

There are many other verses where Allah ﷻ promises His slaves who listen to His instructions, contemplate them, and then push themselves to implement those instructions to the best of their ability, that He ﷻ will take care of them by keeping them away from the harms of these psychological illnesses.

Now, after these definitive promises that Allah ﷻ has taken upon Himself, it is time for us to ask:

How does the Qur'ān treat man and protect him from these illnesses?

Or, if one of these illnesses has subtly infiltrated a person, how does the Qur'ān remove it from his heart?

How can we use the Qur'ān to treat depression?

What are the means of the Qur'ān to keep these promises?

These issues shall be covered in the following chapters, inshAllah.

May Allah the Exalted protect all of us from the diseases of anxiety and psychological unrest.

Chapter Two

The First Cause: Not Knowing the Reality of Life

The first chapter covered the underlying factors behind depression, and they are psychological phenomena. As you know, these factors can be narrowed down to five main causes, and there is no need to repeat them at length in this chapter.

Then, if these are the causes, what is the remedy that is presented by Allah's Book ﷻ? A large number of verses were cited in which Allah ﷻ promises His slaves who pay attention to His teachings and implement the prescription that He ﷻ advises. He promises them that He will protect them from this depression. He promises that He will give them a good life:

He promises that He will remove them from any psychological distress, and there are more verses, many of which were cited in the first chapter.

Towards the end of the first chapter, it was asked: how does Allah's Book implement His promise, which He took upon Himself?

The answer is as follows:

In order to know how Allah's ﷻ Book treats the people who have this illness, or protects them against it, these causes must be kept in mind. Each cause behind this malady has a corresponding remedy in Allah's ﷻ Book.

It would be best to start with the broadest of these causes, which is man's living out this life of his without knowing anything about his reality. He does not know anything about the source of his existence on this earth, or anything about what lies beyond the end that awaits him, which is death. This ignorance, which controls his entire life, is one of the most serious causes of anxiety and psychological unrest.

Before looking at the treatment in Allah's ﷻ Book, it is important to understand the gravity of man's not knowing why he is on this earth.

Imagine, if you will, a person going to sleep at night safe and sound in his bedroom. When he opens his eyes in the morning, he looks and finds that instead of being in his bedroom, in his own house, where he fell asleep, he finds himself in a carriage that is taking him to some unknown destination. His carriage is just one part of a long train. He looks to his right and to his left and nothing is familiar to him. He does not know anything about the direction in which this train is taking him. He does not know the outcome he is heading toward. He does not know anything about any of this. How will this person's state be? Regardless of whether the view that surrounds his train is beautiful and verdant, with aromatic plants, and roses and flowers, or whether the view is the complete opposite, i.e. full of darkness and gloom, and so forth, he will be overcome with anxiety.

'Where am I? How did I get here? Who put me here? Where am I being taken? What decision has been made about me?'

Without doubt, he will be overcome with anxiety, regardless of how many means of gratification, entertainment, and amusement surround him. These means will distract him for some time but he will end up where he was. He will not be able to focus on them for more than a few minutes, after which he will revert to this distress that has overcome him.

This is when his vehicle is actually just one carriage in a train, and when this vehicle only moves around a limited space. What if this train represents one's entire lifespan? What if this train is surrounded by this universe that we are in, by its sprawling planes? How would this person's anxiety be?

Imagine that you open your eyes and look at this life, and you do not know anything about its origin. You do not know if there is a judge who has decreed that you live on this earth for a period of time, or not. You do not know where you come from or where you are going. All you know is the moment that you are in. If you try to look at the past or into the future, you see nothing but a dark unknown.

You could be in a state of wealth or a state of poverty. You could have all the means of entertainment and amusement at your disposal, or you could have nothing of the sort. Whatever state you are in, anxiety will permeate your essence. These questions that are inscribed in your mind and for which you have no answer; they will inevitably, bit by bit, result in depression, anxiety, and psychological unrest.

Man has a natural inclination to love amusement, to love worldly desires and passions, and maybe a person will be distracted and amused when his natural inclination turns towards these things when he is young, in the flower of his youth. Maybe he will be distracted by these amusements and means of forgetfulness, and will not try to answer these burdensome questions that he imposes upon himself.

When youth recedes, however, and these natural inclinations wane, and the autumn of one's life approaches, as represented in middle age and then old age, what will this person's state be? He is not far from departing this life and he still knows nothing about its origin or its outcome. He knows nothing about its roots or its branches. He knows nothing about the reality of death and what happens after death. The means of amusement have now left him behind. The means of entertainment that would respond to his natural inclinations have disappeared, while those same natural inclinations have gone to sleep. How will his state be? In this state, inevitably, depression will start to take hold of him.

Look at secular, materialistic societies. Do not look at the youth who are immersing themselves in all kinds of entertainment and distraction, so that they can be preoccupied from the pain of these questions and not knowing the answers to them. Rather, look at those who are in the autumn of their lives.[10] Those who have lived their youth and then their middle age, and are now in the phases of old age. Look at their circumstances. Sit with them and ask them. Try to extract what is in their souls. You will find depression, and that it has pulverised their feelings. You will find this psychological unrest afflicting their feelings. As they get closer and closer to their final destination, when they will bid farewell to this life, this pain and these feelings just intensify.

This is common knowledge.

What will save a person from this first cause? And how does the Qurʾān prescribe a remedy in order to be cured of it?

The remedy is embodied in this prescription, which consists of the following:

10 Sources: https://www.who.int/news-room/fact-sheets/detail/depression and 'Why depression in old age is different, and how to deal with it – in yourself or a loved one', *South China Morning Post* (Accessed 12 June, 2022).

1) To believe in the Creator of this universe, and to know that this universe has One who constantly sustains it, who created it, and who plans it. There are many different scientific evidences for this right in front of you, and they will nourish your intellect with this faith. If you believe in the Creator ﷻ, you will find yourself at the beginning of a path. This path will save you from depression and from these psychological illnesses.

After you know that this universe has a Creator, that it has a Sustainer who originated and organised it, you then understand that this god has programmed His universe according to a system, and that He has established and assigned you with a task. There is no doubt or uncertainty about this.

2) You believe in Allah ﷻ. The second part of the prescription is that you listen and pay attention to this god that you believe in. You believe in Allah ﷻ and you ask yourself: has any speech from Him reached me? Has any address from Him reached me? Has this god addressed me and identified who He is? You pay attention, you research, you look, and you find yourself standing face to face with Allah's ﷻ address. His Speech is in front of you. What do you read? You read the answers to all of these questions. You read the story of your journey. You read the story of the stages that you progressed through, starting with the first creation all the way through to the conclusion that you shall end at. Allah's ﷻ Book is overflowing with a tender, affectionate, soothing address. It removes you from your estrangement and dreariness and puts you in a meadow of intimacy with these words. Here are some examples.

Look at Allah's ﷻ words when He tells me about man: how he was created, how he progressed, and what his final end and destination is.

﴿وَلَقَدۡ خَلَقۡنَا ٱلۡإِنسَٰنَ مِن سُلَٰلَةٖ مِّن طِينٖ ١٢ ثُمَّ جَعَلۡنَٰهُ نُطۡفَةٗ

فِي قَرَارٖ مَّكِينٖ ١٣ ثُمَّ خَلَقۡنَا ٱلنُّطۡفَةَ عَلَقَةٗ فَخَلَقۡنَا ٱلۡعَلَقَةَ مُضۡغَةٗ

فَخَلَقْنَا ٱلْمُضْغَةَ عِظَٰمًا فَكَسَوْنَا ٱلْعِظَٰمَ لَحْمًا ثُمَّ أَنشَأْنَٰهُ خَلْقًا
ءَاخَرَ ۚ فَتَبَارَكَ ٱللَّهُ أَحْسَنُ ٱلْخَٰلِقِينَ ﴿١٤﴾ ثُمَّ إِنَّكُم بَعْدَ ذَٰلِكَ
لَمَيِّتُونَ ﴿١٥﴾ ثُمَّ إِنَّكُمْ يَوْمَ ٱلْقِيَٰمَةِ تُبْعَثُونَ﴾

"We created man from the purest kind of clay, then made him a drop in a secure receptacle, then formed the drop into a clot and formed the clot into a lump and formed the lump into bones and then clothed the bones in flesh, and then brought him into being as another creature. Blessed is Allah, the Best of Creators! Then subsequently you will certainly die. Then on the Day of Rising you will be raised again." [al-Muʾminūn 23:12-16]

This is Allah's ﷻ answer to your questions. Now, in general, you know the story of your existence in this universe, and you know how existence started and where it will end. You also know that death is not an end, and that you shall return to Allah ﷻ.

Here is another illustration, which is also a tender address from Allah ﷻ to you. It removes this anxiety and its causes from within you. He ﷻ says to you:

﴿يَٰٓأَيُّهَا ٱلْإِنسَٰنُ إِنَّكَ كَادِحٌ إِلَىٰ رَبِّكَ كَدْحًا فَمُلَٰقِيهِ ﴿٦﴾ فَأَمَّا مَنْ أُوتِيَ
كِتَٰبَهُۥ بِيَمِينِهِۦ ﴿٧﴾ فَسَوْفَ يُحَاسَبُ حِسَابًا يَسِيرًا﴾

"O man! You are toiling laboriously towards your Lord but meet Him you will! As for the one who is given his Book in his right hand, he will be given an easy reckoning." [al-Inshiqāq 84:6-8]

"As for the one who is given his Book in his right hand" means the one who does well in his life and his conduct in this world. This is what it means.

﴿فَأَمَّا مَنْ أُوتِيَ كِتَٰبَهُۥ بِيَمِينِهِۦ ۝٧ فَسَوْفَ يُحَاسَبُ حِسَابًا يَسِيرًا ۝٨
وَيَنقَلِبُ إِلَىٰٓ أَهْلِهِۦ مَسْرُورًا﴾

"As for he who is given his Book in his right hand, he will be given an easy reckoning, and return to his family joyfully." [al-Inshiqāq 84:7-9]

This is what Allah ﷻ says.

Therefore, you know that there is a Creator who brought you into existence, and that there is a story behind this journey of yours. Then He ﷻ offers you further assurance and details and says to you:

﴿تَبَٰرَكَ ٱلَّذِى بِيَدِهِ ٱلْمُلْكُ وَهُوَ عَلَىٰ كُلِّ شَىْءٍ قَدِيرٌ ۝١ ٱلَّذِى خَلَقَ
ٱلْمَوْتَ وَٱلْحَيَوٰةَ لِيَبْلُوَكُمْ أَيُّكُمْ أَحْسَنُ عَمَلًا ۚ وَهُوَ ٱلْعَزِيزُ ٱلْغَفُورُ﴾

"Blessed is He who has the Kingdom in His Hand! He has power over all things. He who created death and life to test which of you is best in action. He is the Almighty, the Ever-Forgiving." [al-Mulk 67:1-2]

Then He ﷻ continues elucidating the story of man's journey as well as the function and task that He ﷻ has placed on his neck and entrusted him with.

Then He ﷻ says, uprooting whatever remains of doubt and uncertainty that could be going around man's mind:

﴿أَفَحَسِبْتُمْ أَنَّمَا خَلَقْنَٰكُمْ عَبَثًا وَأَنَّكُمْ إِلَيْنَا لَا تُرْجَعُونَ ۝١١٥
فَتَعَٰلَى ٱللَّهُ ٱلْمَلِكُ ٱلْحَقُّ ۖ لَآ إِلَٰهَ إِلَّا هُوَ رَبُّ ٱلْعَرْشِ ٱلْكَرِيمِ﴾

"Did you suppose that We created you for amusement and that you would not be returned to Us? Exalted is Allah, the King, the Real. There is no god but Him, Lord of the Noble Throne." [al-Muʾminūn 23:115-116]

And He ﷻ also says:

﴿لَوْ أَرَدْنَآ أَن نَّتَّخِذَ لَهْوًا لَّٱتَّخَذْنَٰهُ مِن لَّدُنَّآ إِن كُنَّا فَٰعِلِينَ ﴿١٧﴾ بَلْ نَقْذِفُ بِٱلْحَقِّ عَلَى ٱلْبَٰطِلِ فَيَدْمَغُهُۥ فَإِذَا هُوَ زَاهِقٌ ۚ وَلَكُمُ ٱلْوَيْلُ مِمَّا تَصِفُونَ﴾

"And if We had desired to have some amusement, We would have derived it from Our Presence, but We did not do that. Rather, we hurl the truth against falsehood and it cuts right through it, and it vanishes clean away! Woe without end to you for what you portray" [al-Anbiyāʾ 21:17-18]

In summary, in His ﷻ Book tells us the story of His creation of man, from the dawn of his existence to his end, in which he has an appointment with Allah ﷻ.

He then tells him how to conduct himself in detail. It clarifies the obligations that he must carry out regarding himself, those that he must carry out regarding his Lord, and those that he must carry out regarding his community and his peers.

He ﷻ makes it clear *that man lives this life for the sake of work and effort, and to struggle. As for the reward, it is not today. The reward is tomorrow.* He ﷻ emphasises this and says:

﴿كُلُّ نَفْسٍ ذَآئِقَةُ ٱلْمَوْتِ ۗ وَإِنَّمَا تُوَفَّوْنَ أُجُورَكُمْ يَوْمَ ٱلْقِيَٰمَةِ ۖ فَمَن زُحْزِحَ عَنِ ٱلنَّارِ وَأُدْخِلَ ٱلْجَنَّةَ فَقَدْ فَازَ ۗ وَمَا ٱلْحَيَوٰةُ ٱلدُّنْيَآ إِلَّا مَتَٰعُ ٱلْغُرُورِ﴾

"Every soul will taste death. You will be paid your wages in full on the Day of Rising. Anyone who is distanced from the Fire and admitted to Paradise has triumphed. The life of this world is just the enjoyment of delusion."
[Āl ʿImrān 3:185]

Allah ﷻ gives many parables of this life that we are living. Allah often compares this life to the plants that make the face of this earth green and verdant. This greenery is beautiful to the eyes, and one feels moved. This splendid greenery and its fragrances spread very quickly and cover the surface of these flowers, roses, and so forth. Then, very quickly, it all withers and dies, and these fragrances wane and disappear. Then, when these plants have become dry herbage, a wind comes and blows them away.

The Creator ﷻ gives us a parable of this worldly life; He compares it to this greenery, so that we benefit from its beauty as long as it is there for us, and so that we do not feel sad and pained when it disappears and it is time for us to go.

This is the treatment that Allah ﷻ prescribes for the first cause.

The person whose ignorance has forced him into *this* ignorance, then into depression, and then psychological unrest, will find that which will save him from this depression if he takes this remedy, which Allah ﷻ has prescribed for us.

To corroborate this, there is what was said earlier about elderly people, those who are in the latter stages of their lives. You often find that their faces are replete with the depression that they are feeling, and the reason is what has been mentioned. Look, however, at the people who are at the same stage of their lives in Islamic societies. Look at a person who has passed the stage of youth and then middle age and he is a believer in the Creator ﷻ. He knows that this universe has a Sustainer. He believes in the function for which he was created. He believes in the outcome that awaits him. He deals with Allah ﷻ to the extent of his ability in carrying out these commandments.

Now, he is in old age, and soon, the Angel of Death will come to him and show him out of this world. You will find that his face is beaming. You will find that the serenity in his soul is visible on his face. You will find that he does not care whether his life is prolonged or shortened and finished. He does not care at all. He is just like someone on that train carriage who knows why he is there, he knows what his destination is, and he knows what the final stop is that awaits him. He also knows what he is going to do when he gets off the train. You will not find any sign of this anxiety gripping him, none whatsoever.

The proof of this is that the crime of suicide, or the phenomenon of suicide, afflicts the modern, secular world in a terrible way. The suicide statistics, i.e. the number of people who choose to take their own lives each year, are astonishing.[11] There are many Westerners who study this phenomenon and try to explain its causes and consequences, and they try to find something that psychiatrists can work with, some sort of working theory that they can use to treat their patients.

The truth, however, is that they are in a vicious circle, as many of them have eventually admitted and acknowledged. Why are they in a vicious circle? These Western researchers, who are looking for the secret behind this phenomenon, should look at the fact that most of those who are living the last stages of their lives are beset with depression. This is because they know that they have nothing to do with this world anymore. They mull over their previous dreams. They mull over their youth. Maybe one of these older men will meet one of these older women and they will try to become

11 https://www.who.int/publications/i/item/9789240026643 (Accessed 21 July, 2023).

intimate with one another. They will try to bring back each other's memories of their youth, but it bears no fruit. Physicians try to treat it, but to no avail.

Psychologists try to understand what is behind this, but to no avail. Do you know why? It is because secular, materialistic societies never look for a solution to a problem outside of the material world. They do not look for a way to treat any illness, whatever it may be, outside the material world. This is because they can only see the material world. They only believe in matter. They imagine that this depression has a material cause.

They therefore look at the human body and view it as matter. They look into its essence and its effects but only within the material realm. *They look in the material world for the cause of this depression and they cannot find it.*

Furthermore, maybe they will imagine causes that are not real[12]. Many of them, i.e. psychiatrists, prescribe treatments for their patients, but they are nothing more than neurological medication, medication that treats a material part of man. This medication treats the nerves, and the nerves are a part of matter. It treats the brain, and the brain is a part of matter. The source of this illness is not the nerves. Its source is not the brain. The illness is *reflected* in the nerves. It is *reflected* in the brain. The cause of this illness, however, is something immaterial. The cause is that this person wants to know, wants to understand, why he was put in this life. What is the outcome that awaits him? What is the news? He has lived a period of time and he has eaten, he has drunk, he has entertained himself, he has danced, he has gotten married, and he has enjoyed himself however he pleased, in various ways. Now, he has nothing to do with any of that. Why? What is going on? What is the philosophy that is hidden behind all of this? This is something that

12 Depression is probably not caused by a chemical imbalance in the brain: https://www.ucl.ac.uk/news/2022/jul/analysis-depression-probably-not-caused-chemical-imbalance-brain-new-study (Accessed 08 September, 2022).

is *not* material. The cure for this is with Allah, with the One who created this universe and created this person. Its treatment is to pay attention and listen to the Creator, *after* believing in Him. When he pays attention and listens to Allah ﷻ He will tell him how He created him, by creating his very first ancestor, and how He made man a vicegerent (*khalīfah*) for Allah on this earth:

﴿وَإِذْ قَالَ رَبُّكَ لِلْمَلَٰٓئِكَةِ إِنِّى جَاعِلٌ فِى ٱلْأَرْضِ خَلِيفَةً﴾

"When your Lord said to the angels: 'I am putting a khalīfah in the earth'" [al-Baqarah 2:30]

The remedy is to know the function that one has been created for. The remedy is to know and be reassured that death does not mean non-existence. Rather, after death, one will live a second life, and one's deeds will be displayed and judged. This is the remedy.

Chapter Three
The Second Cause: Fear of the Future

As previously mentioned, the first and most common cause of depression, anxiety and psychological unrest,[13] is when a person does not know anything about the story of his existence and the meaning behind this vast universe that he inhabits. Many of these people, who have turned a blind eye and closed off their intuition to attempt to find an answer to these vital questions, have been exposed and are still being exposed to depression and different types of anxiety and psychological unrest.

The first cause was discussed and there is no need to repeat it at length, but it would be useful to go over its framework in order to move from this first cause to the second one.

The example was given of someone who goes to sleep at night in his own bed and in his own house and when he wakes up, he finds himself on a train that is taking him to some unknown destination. He does not know who has transported him from his house to this train, nor does he know who is driving the train, to which destination the train is heading, and what awaits him at this destination. There is no doubt that this person will experience a great deal of

13 Again, individuals with an anxiety disorder are very likely to meet criteria for a depressive disorder or other psychological disorder.

psychological turmoil no matter how luxurious he views the vehicle to be, and how amiable and beautiful the scenery around him is. His psychological anxiety will overwhelm all this beauty.

However, how lost would his ignorance make him feel if this vehicle were the entire world or universe? This person opens his eyes and finds himself in a world without knowing what or who got him there. He does not know the purpose of his existence. He sees people living and then dying, and he does not know what death is. He does not know what awaits him after death. This chain of ignorance creates dangerous causes, which today we call depression, anxiety, and psychological unrest.

Usually, a person in his youth will try to avoid these vital questions by resorting to entertainment and chasing amusements, which takes up all his time. Because he lacks knowledge, he tries to stay far away from these questions and the unease of attempting to answer them. Most young people who excessively seek entertainment and heedless distractions do so in order to forget these vital questions that keep chasing them.

Imagine, however, when the phase of youth ends followed by the phase of middle age, in which desires, whims, and basic instincts recede. This is then followed by the stage of old age with its darkness, these questions must then dominate and conquer the mind and self. Where, then, can this person escape from these questions? The time for desires is over. He no longer has the capability or means to follow his whims, and so these questions must dominate at this time. You might notice that depression dominates the middle aged and the elderly in secular, materialistic societies in a persistent and dangerous manner because the time of resorting to heedless distractions and entertainment has passed. There is only one thing they can resort to: intoxication through drugs and alcohol. For any age group, this can be a temporary solution, but it is like curing one disease with another.

How does the Qurʾān cure the root cause of the problem?

As was stated previously, the Qurʾān cures this problem by placing one in front of the healing answers to these incessant questions:

Who am I? Why was I created and put in this life?

Where am I heading? What is my final destination?

What is death? What will I face after death?

What is the duty that I have been assigned in this life, if any?

The Qurʾān places you in front of detailed answers to all these questions. The starting point to these answers is the belief that the One addressing you is Allah and the certainty that the One speaking to you is the Creator of this universe, your Creator, the One who created life and death and what comes after life and death.

When you are certain that these are His words, you must believe those words. And so, when you listen to the schedule of this "journey" from start to finish, the story of your existence and your duty, you will be relieved of the factors that lead to anxiety and depression.

The Qurʾān is full of verses that help man by placing him in front of the information that he desperately thirsts for. For example, look at the verse:

﴿يَٰٓأَيُّهَا ٱلۡإِنسَٰنُ إِنَّكَ كَادِحٌ إِلَىٰ رَبِّكَ كَدۡحٗا فَمُلَٰقِيهِ ٦ فَأَمَّا
مَنۡ أُوتِيَ كِتَٰبَهُۥ بِيَمِينِهِۦ ٧ فَسَوۡفَ يُحَاسَبُ حِسَابٗا يَسِيرٗا ٨
وَيَنقَلِبُ إِلَىٰٓ أَهۡلِهِۦ مَسۡرُورٗا ٩ وَأَمَّا مَنۡ أُوتِيَ كِتَٰبَهُۥ وَرَآءَ ظَهۡرِهِۦ ١٠
فَسَوۡفَ يَدۡعُواْ ثُبُورٗا ١١ وَيَصۡلَىٰ سَعِيرًا﴾

"O Man! You are toiling laboriously towards your Lord but meet Him you will! As for him who is given his Book in his right hand, he will be given an easy reckoning and return to his family joyfully. But as for him who is given his Book behind his back, he will cry out for destruction but will be roasted in a Searing Blaze."
[al-Inshiqāq 84:6-12]

These words are repeated in the Qurʾān, for example in the verses:

﴿وَأَن لَّيْسَ لِلْإِنسَٰنِ إِلَّا مَا سَعَىٰ ﴿٣٩﴾ وَأَنَّ سَعْيَهُۥ سَوْفَ يُرَىٰ ﴿٤٠﴾ ثُمَّ يُجْزَىٰهُ ٱلْجَزَآءَ ٱلْأَوْفَىٰ ﴿٤١﴾ وَأَنَّ إِلَىٰ رَبِّكَ ٱلْمُنتَهَىٰ ﴿٤٢﴾ وَأَنَّهُۥ هُوَ أَضْحَكَ وَأَبْكَىٰ ﴿٤٣﴾ وَأَنَّهُۥ هُوَ أَمَاتَ وَأَحْيَا﴾

"That man will have nothing but what he strives for; that his striving will most certainly be seen; that he will then receive repayment of the fullest kind; that the ultimate end is with your Lord; that it is He Who brings about both laughter and tears; that it is He Who brings about both death and life" [an-Najm 53:39-44]

That was the theory. Now for the practice.

Can you find someone who truly believes in Allah, who truly believes that these are His words, and has been swept away by this type of depression or by these factors that lead to anxiety and psychological unrest?

You will not be able to find this.

However, look at people in secular, materialistic societies and specifically at those who have passed the stage of youth into middle age and then old age. Try to observe their state for some time.

Can you see how much anxiety and psychological pain they are in? Look at their facial expressions. Are they not overflowing with depression?

The reason for this is that they live in nostalgia of their youth, remembering the alluring desires and whims that they embraced. But now, all this has passed. The play mat has been stowed away and those playful nights are long gone. The bright lights under which they played are now absent. It has all faded and disappeared. When one of them looks to the future, he does not find anything but darkness on the horizon and the spectre of death approaching him. He looks and sees that any meaning to his life is slipping away.

Where is he going? What will happen after he dies?

He does not know anything about this.

As for the believer, he is far removed from all of this. The Muslim who truly knows his Lord and the story of life cannot be afflicted with this type of depression in any way.

This was the first cause, and this was its cure. Many of Allah's verses, in which He talks to man with speech dipped in mercy and kindness to get him out of his ignorance and to protect him against depression, have been presented.

Fear of Failure in the Future

Let us now look at the second cause of depression, anxiety, and psychological unrest.

The second cause is the fear of failure. Fear of failure can be in the academic field or in any work or endeavour for the sake of sustenance, such as business, trade, agriculture, manufacturing, and so on. Fear of failure can also be in the search for riches or the escape from poverty.

Fear of failure can also be when someone finds himself indulged in sin without having any hope of Allah's forgiveness.

The common denominator here is fear of future failure. This is the second cause and one of the main sources of psychological anxiety.

This cause needs to be explained first, and then its cure.

Assume, may Allah forbid, that your heart is devoid of faith in Allah and that your conviction is bereft of belief and trust in Him. Therefore, when you are young and you go to school, you look at the people around you and you notice that some are successful in their education while others fail. You therefore think to yourself:

'Will I be of the former group or the latter? If I am part of the failing group, what will my life be like? How can I build a future for myself and my family, and how will I achieve my desires and ambitions? What can guarantee that I will be successful and not a failure?'

If these worries constantly surround you and you repeatedly give in to them, they will eventually take root inside of you and turn into a type of depression and anxiety.

This is the case when your soul is devoid of belief and trust in Allah.

Another example would be if you started projects in order to earn a living and strived to be rich. Obviously, this kind of work involves some risk.

'Will I be successful like my peers and be able to compete with them or will I be a complete failure?'

'Who will tell me the future? Who will tell me what is going to happen? If the result is failure, how will I compensate for all this money that I ventured with and invested to reach my goal, and what will be the outcome?'

And that is how you build different kinds of imaginary scenarios based on unreal fears that fill your head. Your heart is bereft of any certainty that Allah exists and of the belief that whoever relies on Allah, He is sufficient for him.

When the heart is devoid of this, anxiety takes complete control.

At first, the anxiety is normal even though it is painful. For example, when you return home and try to go to bed, you will toss and turn. It is normal to toss and turn in bed for a while without any sleep because you are thinking about the outcomes of your endeavours throughout the day.

'What will be the end result of this project? How will this project affect my situation?'

Then, eventually, after all that worrying and stressing, Allah blesses you with sleep.

However, the moment you wake up, those visions immediately return to your mind once again. Furthermore, if this anxiety lasts for longer periods and especially if your endeavours end in failure, contrary to what you expected, then undoubtedly you will be in a state of shock. This will then trigger a type of depression that can lead to psychological anxiety.

This is well known. The person who constantly fears the spectre of poverty always embraces the dreams of richness, and eagerly strives in search of wealth in his life, if not for himself then for his children whom he will leave behind. When this person has a soul devoid of trust in Allah and a mind lacking certainty that Allah ﷻ is the one directing this entire universe, he ruminates this situation with huge pains and suffers as a result. The spectre of poverty hardly ever leaves him alone.

'Will I eventually win my fight against poverty and be among the rich, who are happy and having fun in their exclusive circles, or will I always be poor?'

The spectre of poverty always accompanies him. What would be his condition if poverty actually struck him every once in a while? What if his business endeavours fail him and he consequently finds himself among the poor, and remains that way indefinitely? What will be his mental state then?

This is another cause of anxiety and turmoil in the soul.

How many people are there in such situations, people who have been overwhelmed with depression due to mere illusions, which, of course, do not exist?

This was a detailed image of this second cause, which is the fear of failure in the future.

What is the cure?

The cure is in the Book of Allah ﷻ.

Go back and contemplate the Lord's Speech and you will find the cure for all illnesses of this nature.

What does Allah ﷻ tell you?

First, He commands you to work and not to resort to idleness or unemployment. He tells you:

﴿هُوَ ٱلَّذِى جَعَلَ لَكُمُ ٱلْأَرْضَ ذَلُولًا فَٱمْشُوا فِى مَنَاكِبِهَا وَكُلُوا مِن رِّزْقِهِۦ ۖ وَإِلَيْهِ ٱلنُّشُورُ﴾

"It is He who made the earth submissive to you, so walk its broad trails and eat what it provides. The Resurrection is to Him." [al-Mulk 67:15]

In all the verses in which Allah commands righteous deeds, the term 'righteous deeds'[14] means that the first thing you do is work for the sake of sustenance, agriculture, farming, manufacturing, and trade. All these are works that Allah commands us to do.

The Prophet ﷺ, in the authentic ḥadīth, further supports, explains, and analyses the meaning of these verses when he says to us:

{The strong believer is better and more beloved to Allah than the weak believer, although both are good. Strive for that which will benefit you, seek the help of Allah, and do not feel helpless. If something afflicts you, do not say: 'If only I had done such-and-such, the matter would be such-and-such'. Rather, say: 'Allah has predestined, and whatever He wants, He does.' Indeed, 'if only' opens a door for Shayṭān to work.}[15]

Allah ﷻ first commands you to work in all the ways that build a civilised and materially viable society.

Then, after you answer Allah's ﷻ call and say: 'Here I am O' Lord, I have come out of my home to work and to earn a living', He reassures you, by saying:

﴿وَمَن يَتَوَكَّلْ عَلَى ٱللَّهِ فَهُوَ حَسْبُهُۥٓ﴾

14 Ar. *aʿmāl ṣāliḥah.*

15 *Sunan Ibn Mājah,* Ḥadīth no. 79.

"Whoever puts his trust in Allah – He will be enough for him."
[at-Ṭalāq 65:3]

It is as if Allah is saying: 'Now that you have started working, plant in your heart My trust. Your work is not what maintains your livelihood, your business is not what makes you happy, and your work on the land, growing crops and raising animals, is not what enriches you and provides for you, rather it is Me. I command the land to respond to your agriculture. I command the different factors and creations to yield to your work and efforts. Put your trust in Me after you have taken the first step and carried out what you were supposed to.'

"Whoever puts his trust in Allah – He will be enough for him."

Furthermore, Allah says:

﴿وَمَن يَتَّقِ ٱللَّهَ يَجْعَل لَّهُۥ مَخْرَجًا ۝٢ وَيَرْزُقْهُ
مِنْ حَيْثُ لَا يَحْتَسِبُ﴾

"Whoever has fear[16] of Allah – He will give him a way out and provide for him from where he does not expect."
[at-Ṭalāq 65:2-3]

In other words: 'Obey My commands, reconcile with Me, and trust in Me. Then, leave the result of your work to Me. I am the guarantor of your happiness.'

﴿مَنْ عَمِلَ صَٰلِحًا مِّن ذَكَرٍ أَوْ أُنثَىٰ وَهُوَ مُؤْمِنٌ
فَلَنُحْيِيَنَّهُۥ حَيَوٰةً طَيِّبَةً﴾

"Anyone who acts rightly, male or female, being a believer, We will give them a good life" [an-Naḥl 16:97]

16 Ar. *taqwā*.

Moreover, the Prophet ﷺ clarifies and explains these verses and reminds you to be connected to Allah ﷻ through awareness, observation, and trust, and that the means to helping you achieve this is plenty of remembrance[17] in its various forms. He ﷺ says in his authentic ḥadīths:

{Whoever seeks Allah's forgiveness constantly, Allah will grant him relief from every distress, a way out from every adversity, and will provide him sustenance from where he does not expect.}[18]

Allah ﷻ has addressed you with words that are overflowing with definitive promises: if man responds to the commands of Allah and exerts the efforts required from him, then trusts in Allah, relies and depends on Him, Allah will provide for him.

Imagine you are a believer in Allah, trusting in the speech directed to you from Allah, and believing what He said:

"Whoever has fear of Allah – He will give him a way out and provide for him."

You will thus go out and work hard, and then you will return home and sleep well because you have fulfilled the condition that Allah has commanded of you while leaving all other things to Him, and you know that He will support you.

Can depression consequently seep into your heart?

Never!

17 Ar. *dhikr*.

18 Imam Yahya an-Nawawi, *Riyadh as-Saliheen* (Jeddah: Dar al-Minhaj, 2015/1436), 596. Ḥadīth no.1912.

Chapter Four
The Third Cause:
Fear of Adversity & Affliction

The third cause of depression is the grief and worry that befalls a person because he fears the afflictions that he can see around him, and which beset different people.

Therefore, grief and worry because one fears affliction is a third cause of depression and psychological unrest. This grief and worry either comes about as a result of fearing that affliction will grip one in the future, or it comes about because of an affliction that one is actually in.

What is mean by "afflictions"[19] are the various, different illnesses, and general afflictions that entire countires and nations are exposed to. This is either because of wars, and other manmade disasters, or because of divine will: earthquakes and the like, which some people call "natural disasters". They can be called "divine matters"; they come from Allah ﷻ.

There are people who are highly sensitive. In their current circumstances, you find them far removed from afflictions. One of them enjoys perfect health and well-being. He does not suffer from anything that would disturb him psychologically. He does not suffer from any deformity or disfigurement. He does not suffer from anything that would cause sorrow or distress. The community that

19 Ar. *maṣāʾib*.

he lives in is also one of prosperity. The country that he lives in is protected by Allah's providence. Despite all of that, grief and worry have beset him. Why?

It is because yesterday, he visited someone and found that this person had been struck with some terrible illness. He then went home and imagined that maybe he would be struck with the same illness tomorrow. Then what would he do? If he were struck with this illness, how would he rid himself of it? How could he protect himself from being struck with it in the first place?

Or he hears news that an affliction has struck some country, that an earthquake has killed many people and destroyed many houses. He hears lots of news like this. He goes back home and he imagines: what if an affliction like this strikes us as well?

People like this are highly sensitive and they imagine these things, and it cannot be said that being highly sensitive is a blessing or a punishment.

Then, when an actual affliction strikes, anything is to be expected in terms of anxiety, psychological unrest, and depression. An accident happens. He loses his right eye, for example. He used to have a normal body. He used to see with two, beautiful eyes, and now he is disfigured. He goes back to his house with a feeling of endless grief and sorrow, a feeling of unmitigated pain. This is because this affliction has happened.

Another example is a man who keeps asking himself: 'Will I remain free of illness, far away from epidemics?' Then, all of sudden, he feels some pain in his body, some twinge in his chest, for example. Then, before consulting a doctor, he is struck with another illness, which is the illness of scruples and doubts, the illness of anxiety.

What do you think will happen if, after various scans and tests, it becomes clear that some illness, malignant or not, is found in his body? He is then attacked by feelings of anxiety and depression. The person comes to be in a state in which he hates the life that he is blessed with. He is not able to seek refuge in death because he does not know what death is, and he does not know what comes after death. At the same time, he is not able to keep his composure and function properly.

This event constitutes a well-known and widespread cause of depression and psychological unrest. Who is it that is exposed to such banes? It is the one who is veiled from Allah. It is the one who is veiled from Allah's Book ﷻ. It is the one who does not make time to study Allah's ﷻ address to him. If he were to turn to Allah's address, after believing in Him, Allah would save him from this depression and from this pain.

Such a person would find himself living in a fortified fortress, very far removed from the arrows of these illnesses.

What does Allah ﷻ tell us? The Creator ﷻ says:

﴿مَآ أَصَابَ مِن مُّصِيبَةٍ فِي ٱلْأَرْضِ وَلَا فِيٓ أَنفُسِكُمْ إِلَّا فِي كِتَٰبٍ مِّن قَبْلِ أَن نَّبْرَأَهَآ ۚ إِنَّ ذَٰلِكَ عَلَى ٱللَّهِ يَسِيرٌ ۝٢٢ لِّكَيْلَا تَأْسَوْا۟ عَلَىٰ مَا فَاتَكُمْ وَلَا تَفْرَحُوا۟ بِمَآ ءَاتَىٰكُمْ ۗ وَٱللَّهُ لَا يُحِبُّ كُلَّ مُخْتَالٍ فَخُورٍ﴾

"Nothing happens, either in the earth or in yourselves, without its being in a Book before We make it happen. That is something easy for Allah. That is so that you will not be grieved about the things that pass you by or exult about the things that come to you. Allah does not love any vain or boastful man." [al-Ḥadīd 57: 22-23]

These words need to be listened to after one believes in Allah. That is, one believes that the one saying these words is Allah ﷻ.

What do these words mean?

They mean that when the Creator ﷻ created man and everything else, He laid out the various paths that this man would follow. He laid out the events that would happen to this man. He organised and decreed all the matters in which he has a choice in and in which he does not, as well as everything that he will be exposed to. *Allah has decreed His decree.*

"Nothing happens, - this is what Allah ﷻ says - **either in the earth or in yourselves, without its being in a Book before We make it happen."** i.e. before We bring it into existence. It is all organised and set up. **"That is so that you will not be grieved about the things that pass you by or exult about the things that come to you. Allah does not love any vain or boastful man."**

The meaning of *farḥ* (exult) is to be conceited, to be haughty, and to be arrogant.

When I read these words, the matter is concluded. There is no need for me to be excessively cautious. There is no need for excessive planning. I do what Allah has commanded:

﴿وَقُلِ ٱعْمَلُوا فَسَيَرَى ٱللَّهُ عَمَلَكُمْ﴾

"Act, for Allah will see your actions." [at-Tawbah 9:105]

﴿هُوَ ٱلَّذِى جَعَلَ لَكُمُ ٱلْأَرْضَ ذَلُولًا فَٱمْشُوا فِى مَنَاكِبِهَا﴾

"It is He who made the earth submissive to you, so walk its broad trails." [al-Mulk 67:15]

This is what Allah ﷻ has said. Allah has commanded you to be prepared, but you will not be excessive, because you know that what Allah ﷻ has decreed will happen, and therefore it is not for you, as a created person, to presume that you can ward something off from yourself. You cannot ward off anything.

You carry out, however, a function that Allah has commanded you to.

Is this treatment sufficient? No, it is not sufficient. This is just one prescription, and it must be combined with other prescriptions. This prescription alone will not suffice, because someone might say, 'Fine. I know that the affliction that is coming will inevitably come, because Allah has decreed such. But how can I receive it? How can I accept it wholeheartedly and not be worried about it?'

This is where the other treatment comes in. In His Book, Allah ﷻ tells you about it in many words, and they are lengthy and versatile in their expression. He tells you about the lowliness of this life and its lack of importance, and that man should not make much of what is good about it or be saddened by what is bad about it. This is because it is only a road leading to a final destination. This is repeated many times in Allah's Book. For example, He ﷻ says:

﴿ٱعْلَمُوٓا۟ أَنَّمَا ٱلْحَيَوٰةُ ٱلدُّنْيَا لَعِبٌ وَلَهْوٌ وَزِينَةٌ وَتَفَاخُرٌۢ بَيْنَكُمْ وَتَكَاثُرٌ
فِى ٱلْأَمْوَٰلِ وَٱلْأَوْلَـٰدِ ۖ كَمَثَلِ غَيْثٍ أَعْجَبَ ٱلْكُفَّارَ نَبَاتُهُۥ ثُمَّ يَهِيجُ فَتَرَىٰهُ
مُصْفَرًّا ثُمَّ يَكُونُ حُطَـٰمًا ۖ وَفِى ٱلْـَٔاخِرَةِ عَذَابٌ شَدِيدٌ وَمَغْفِرَةٌ مِّنَ ٱللَّهِ
وَرِضْوَٰنٌ ۚ وَمَا ٱلْحَيَوٰةُ ٱلدُّنْيَآ إِلَّا مَتَـٰعُ ٱلْغُرُورِ ۝٢٠ سَابِقُوٓا۟ إِلَىٰ مَغْفِرَةٍ مِّن
رَّبِّكُمْ وَجَنَّةٍ عَرْضُهَا كَعَرْضِ ٱلسَّمَآءِ وَٱلْأَرْضِ أُعِدَّتْ لِلَّذِينَ ءَامَنُوا۟ بِٱللَّهِ
وَرُسُلِهِۦ ۚ ذَٰلِكَ فَضْلُ ٱللَّهِ يُؤْتِيهِ مَن يَشَآءُ ۚ وَٱللَّهُ ذُو ٱلْفَضْلِ ٱلْعَظِيمِ﴾

"Know that the life of this world is merely a game and a diversion and ostentation and a cause of boasting among yourselves and trying to outdo one another in wealth and children: like the plant-growth after rain that delights the cultivators, but then it withers and you see it turning yellow, and then it becomes broken stubble. In the Hereafter there is terrible punishment but also forgiveness from Allah and His good pleasure. The life of this world is nothing but the enjoyment of delusion. Race each other to forgiveness from your Lord and to a Garden whose breadth is like that of heaven and earth combined, made ready for those who believe in Allah and His Messengers. This is Allah's favour, which He gives to those He wills. Allah's favour is indeed immense." [al-Ḥadīd 57: 20-21]

You have to allow yourself to be sated by these words, which are oft-repeated in Allah's ﷻ Book. Another example is when Allah says these words on the tongue of a believer from the people of Firʿawn:

﴿يَـٰقَوْمِ إِنَّمَا هَـٰذِهِ ٱلْحَيَوٰةُ ٱلدُّنْيَا مَتَـٰعٌ وَإِنَّ ٱلْـَٔاخِرَةَ هِىَ دَارُ ٱلْقَرَارِ﴾

"My people! The life of this world is only fleeting enjoyment. It is the Hereafter that is the abode of permanence." [Ghāfir 40:39]

﴿فَسَتَذْكُرُونَ مَآ أَقُولُ لَكُمْ ۚ وَأُفَوِّضُ أَمْرِىٓ إِلَى ٱللَّهِ ۚ إِنَّ ٱللَّهَ بَصِيرٌۢ بِٱلْعِبَادِ﴾

"You will remember what I am telling you. I consign my destiny completely to Allah. Truly Allah sees His slaves." [Ghāfir 40:44]

If you allow yourself to be sated by these words, your estimation of this world will decrease and then continue to decrease, down from its lofty rank that used to hold sway over you. You will look at it and you will find that it is indeed insignificant. It is just an intermission. It is like a break that you take and then you move on. Of course, you try to protect this break from anything that would disturb it, or from any sort of tribulation, because that obviously pains you.

When an affliction happens, however, you will, first of all, see it as something minor, because you know that it happened within a time that has no value. It has no importance. This is the *dunyā*, i.e. the lowest life, the lowest; you will depart from it and settle somewhere great, so great that it will make you forget everything that happened in this life.

When this affliction happens, after you have allowed yourself to be sated by these words that Allah ﷻ has said to you, this affliction will shrink in size, regardless of whether it is an illness, poverty, disfigurement, an accident, an amputation...whatever it is, it will not affect you in that way. Yes, you will feel pain, there is no doubt, but something better will overcome whatever it is that you are feeling.

Secondly, go back to the first prescription. It is something that Allah has decreed, and you believe in Allah. You believe that He is the Creator. He is the One who plans everything. Then you believe that Allah is kind, that Allah is loving, that Allah is most merciful. You are confident in all of this.

This affliction has come to you from this god, in this *lowest* life.

First of all, you are certain that this affliction, at least outwardly, is indeed an affliction and a heavy blow. However, there must be a blessing inside of it, and if Allah did not want to nurture you, better you and ennoble you by way of it, He would not have sent it your way. This is because you are confident that Allah is most merciful. You are confident that Allah is kind.

How many accidents look like afflictions but are actually blessings?

You are confident that Allah is wise; He puts matters in their proper place. He is most merciful, kind, and loving.

Therefore, when you see that an accident has happened – may Allah protect us all – to your house, to your person, to your progeny, to your spouse, to the environment around you, you immediately remember Allah's ﷻ words:

﴿وَعَسَىٰٓ أَن تَكْرَهُوا شَيْـًٔا وَهُوَ خَيْرٌ لَّكُمْ ۖ وَعَسَىٰٓ أَن تُحِبُّوا شَيْـًٔا وَهُوَ شَرٌّ لَّكُمْ ۗ وَٱللَّهُ يَعْلَمُ وَأَنتُمْ لَا تَعْلَمُونَ﴾

"It may be that you hate something when it is good for you, and it may be that you love something when it is bad for you. Allah knows and you do not know." [al-Baqarah 2:216]

You immediately remember Allah's ﷻ words:

﴿وَأَسْبَغَ عَلَيْكُمْ نِعَمَهُۥ ظَٰهِرَةً وَبَاطِنَةً﴾

"And He has showered His blessings upon you, both outwardly and inwardly." [Luqmān 31:20]

What is the inward blessing? It is the blessing that is wrapped in afflictions. It is an affliction in its outward form, but if you were to pierce it, and let some time pass, you would find that there was a wisdom behind why it happened.

This is confidence in Allah; your certainty that Allah is wise, your certainty that your affliction was planned in Allah's knowledge. It was inevitable that it would happen. You will not say to yourself: 'If only I had not done that.' 'If only I had planned properly.' 'If only I had taken precautions.' 'If I had taken those precautions that I was talking about, this would not have happened.' This is what tears up one's insides. This is what forces one into a state of psychological unrest.

You will not say things like this. Instead, you will remember the words of Allah's Messenger ﷺ in an authentic ḥadīth: {If something afflicts you, do not say: 'If only I had done such-and-such, the matter would be such-and-such'. Rather, say: 'Allah has predestined, and whatever He wants, He does.' Indeed, 'if only' opens a door for Shayṭān to work.}[20] How beautiful are these words.

Do not give in to saying 'if only': 'If only I had done this', 'If only I had taken steps to prevent such-and-such', 'If only I had followed the advice of so-and-so, the situation would be such-and-such.'

When you give in to saying 'if only', you open a door for Shayṭān to work. What is Shayṭān's work?[21] It is the depression that Shayṭān puts inside you. It is the anxiety that Shayṭān uses to hold sway over you.

When you have grasped this reality, you have removed yourself from the spectres of these afflictions, and you have liberated yourself from a great deal of their impact, not all of it, but a great deal of it.

The third prescription is to rely on similar words from Allah ﷻ, who says:

﴿وَلَنَبْلُوَنَّكُم بِشَيْءٍ مِّنَ ٱلْخَوْفِ وَٱلْجُوعِ وَنَقْصٍ مِّنَ ٱلْأَمْوَٰلِ
وَٱلْأَنفُسِ وَٱلثَّمَرَٰتِ ۗ وَبَشِّرِ ٱلصَّٰبِرِينَ ﴿١٥٥﴾ ٱلَّذِينَ إِذَآ أَصَٰبَتْهُم مُّصِيبَةٌ

20 Related by Muslim, no. 2664.
وإن أصابَك شيءٌ فلا تقلْ : لو أني فعلتُ لكانَ كذا وكذا ، ولكن قلْ قدَّرَ اللهُ وما شاءَ فعلَ فإن لو تفتحُ عملَ الشيطانِ.

21 See Appendix C for further details.

قَالُوٓا۟ إِنَّا لِلَّهِ وَإِنَّآ إِلَيْهِ رَٰجِعُونَ ﴿١٥٦﴾ أُو۟لَـٰٓئِكَ عَلَيْهِمْ صَلَوَٰتٌ مِّن رَّبِّهِمْ وَرَحْمَةٌ ۖ وَأُو۟لَـٰٓئِكَ هُمُ ٱلْمُهْتَدُونَ﴾

"We will test you with a certain amount of fear and hunger and loss of wealth and life and fruits. But give good news to the steadfast. Those who, when disaster strikes them, say: 'We belong to Allah and to Him we shall return.' Those are the people who will have blessings and mercy from their Lord; they are the ones who are guided."
[al-Baqarah 2:155-157]

This is the third prescription. Combine these prescriptions and see what happens. Will feelings of depression afflict you? Never.

What is the reality behind this third prescription? The meaning of these words is that Allah is saying: 'Listen, son of Adam. You have come into this lowest life and you are subject to My conditions. You do not come into this worldly life and impose your own conditions. You are created, and you live and grow within this lowest life. The conditions, upon whose foundations you were brought into existence, are as follows:

'You will not find permanent, constant happiness in this life. You will not find that the nature of this life is based on the foundations of giving precedence to everything you desire and covet. Never. The nature of this life, which I have established you in, is not like that. The life that I have established you in, by My decision, is a mixture of ease and hardship,[22] good days and bad days, good and evil, that which is pleasing and that which is displeasing. I have a brilliant wisdom in that. I have established you in a life that follows this approach.'

This is the meaning of:

22 See Āl ʿImrān 3:134: *as-sarā' wa aḍ-ḍarā'*.

"We will test you with a certain amount – a certain amount – **of fear and hunger and loss of wealth and life..."**

'From now on, you should know the nature of the life that I have established you in. However you may try, you will never be able to extricate yourself from the system that I have placed you in, in this life.

'And I have a brilliant wisdom therein. I created you on this earth so that you would implement your slavehood to Me, and so that I would reward you, *after* death; if good then good and if bad then bad. You cannot implement the reality of slavehood unless it is on an earth in which good is mixed with bad. When you find good, you are grateful. When you come across bad, you are patient. Patience is an expression of slavehood to Me and gratitude is another expression of slavehood to Me.

'When a person departs from this world and comes back to Me but he is not carrying a testimony of his gratitude when he was in blessings nor a testimony of his patience when he was in hardship, this person has not implemented My right of slavehood over Him in any way, shape, or form.'

This is the wisdom behind this life being a mixture of good and bad.

When you pay attention and listen to these words, you surrender to Allah's ﷻ judgement. Then there is the conclusion:

But give good news to the steadfast. Those who, when disaster strikes them, say: 'We belong to Allah...'

Inna lillāh. Think about these words, these amazing, divine words. They say: 'We belong to Allah.' In other words, I am not my own property. I am my Lord's property. He does whatever He wants with me.

'...and to Him we shall return.' Our return is to Allah ﷻ. This is just a path leading to Him.

Allah ﷻ teaches us how to be content, how to be patient, and how to be confident that Allah is wise in what He does. Then, what does He say?

Those are the people who will have blessings and mercy from their Lord; they are the ones who are guided."

This is an immense glad tidings from Allah. Imagine the person who is familiar with the nature of this life, as Allah has explained it, first of all, and then understands man's duty when he is tested with an affliction, which is to be patient, to be content, and to say to Allah. 'I am your property, my Lord, and I shall return to You. You do whatever You want with me. You dispose of your property.' Is it possible for this person to be struck with depression? By Allah, besides Whom there is no other god, no.

His state will be like that of our master Muʿādh[23] ؓ when he was on his deathbed. When the pangs of death had started and he was in agony, he opened his eyes and went into an intimate conversation with Allah. He said: 'O Lord, choke me to death, for by Your might, You know that my heart loves You.'[24]

23 He is Muʿadh ibn Jabal, al-Anṣārī al-Khazrajī, Abū ʿAbdir Raḥmān, the foremost scholar in knowledge of the lawful and the unlawful according to the testimony of the Messenger of Allah ﷺ when he said, {The most knowledgeable of my Ummah regarding the lawful and the unlawful is Muʿādh ibn Jabal.} He was a handsome youth, and out of all the youth of the Helpers, he was the best of them in terms of forbearance, munificence, and modesty. He embraced Islam at the age of 18, and witnessed ʿAqabah, Badr, and all subsequent battles. The Messenger ﷺ sent him to be in charge of Yemen. He died in the prime of his youth as a fighter in the year 18 AH from the plague of ʿAmwās (Emmaus) at the age of 34. 157 ḥadīth have been related on his authority from the Messenger of Allah ﷺ. Please see the biographies listed at the end of *Al-Wāfī: A Thorough Commentary on the Forty Nawāwiyyah.*

24 اخْنُقْنِي خَنْقَكَ، فَوَعِزَّتِكَ إِنَّكَ لَتَعْلَمُ أَنَّ قَلْبِي يُحِبُّكَ

Look at that. Faith in Allah. Confidence in Allah. Knowledge of the nature of this life. Knowledge of what Allah has prepared for those who are patient. All of this melts and pulverises afflictions. This is the third prescription.

The first prescription is to know that all afflictions, before they came, were decreed and ordered. Therefore, what is the benefit of this prescription? The benefit of this prescription is that you know that you should not say: 'If only I had done such-and-such, this affliction would not have happened', 'If only I had planned properly, I would not have suffered this loss', 'If only I had taken the following precaution, this accident would not have happened.' You do not say anything like this. This is because you know that this affliction must happen. If it does not happen because of this reason, Allah will create another reason. This, therefore, saves you from a portion of unrest and depression.

The second prescription is to know the insignificance of this life, and that this is not the life that you should embrace. It is not the life that you should regard as everything, as if there were nothing coming after it. This is what you find, for example, in Allah's words:

"Know that the life of this world is merely a game and a diversion and ostentation and a cause of boasting among yourselves and trying to outdo one another in wealth and children – then what does He say? He says: **"like the plant-growth after rain that delights the cultivators, but then it withers** [26:54] **and** – very soon, after only a short period of time - **you see it turning yellow, and then it becomes broken stubble."** It falls to pieces, winds come from the east and west and blow it about, and then there is nothing but traces left. This is a very accurate illustration.

"The life of this world is nothing but the enjoyment of delusion."

That is the second prescription, and you can add it to the first prescription.

The third prescription is what Allah ﷻ says to you in His Book, and which the poet summarises by saying:

This abode, if it makes you laugh one day

Tomorrow, that same abode will make you weep.

And if it makes you weep one day, it will make you laugh tomorrow.

Good is always mixed with bad. There are many verses in Allah's Speech that demonstrate this:

﴿لَتُبْلَوُنَّ فِىٓ أَمْوَٰلِكُمْ وَأَنفُسِكُمْ﴾

"You will be tested in your wealth and in yourselves..." [Āl ʿImrān 3:186]

﴿وَلَنَبْلُوَنَّكُم بِشَىْءٍ مِّنَ ٱلْخَوْفِ وَٱلْجُوعِ وَنَقْصٍ مِّنَ ٱلْأَمْوَٰلِ وَٱلْأَنفُسِ وَٱلثَّمَرَٰتِ ۗ وَبَشِّرِ ٱلصَّٰبِرِينَ﴾

"We will test you with a certain amount of fear and hunger and loss of wealth and life and fruits. But give good news to the steadfast. [al-Baqarah 2:155]

So what should you expect from this life? Should you expect everything to be beautiful? Should you expect to be happy all the time, and that everything will go your way? If you expect that, you will be on a collision course with the opposite. You know the nature of this world, based on what Allah has told you.

Then what?

He has promised you that if you are patient, if you are content, and you adorn yourself with contentment with Allah ﷻ He will grant you, on the heels of this affliction, indescribable bliss.

The value and worth of knowing this will appear immediately. This person will not be shocked or surprised by some huge affliction the same way it afflicts those who are ignorant of Allah. Never.

"Imagine two people living under the same roof and experiencing the same calamity, one is a believer and the other is not. The affliction is the same. The affliction will pulverise the one who is removed from Allah, and as a result, the aforementioned illnesses will strike him. The other will sleep peacefully, and say: 'My Lord, You have decreed and I am content. This worldly life is just a road. I know you will compensate me with something good.'

May Allah fill our hearts with faith in Him, with confidence in His wisdom, and His mercy.

There is still a lot more to discuss.

Chapter Five
The Third Cause (Continued): Fear of Adversity & Affliction - Having No Hope of Forgiveness

It has been explained that the third cause of depression is distress or unease due to the fear of being afflicted with the calamities that one sees others suffering from or going through, whatever these calamities may be: financial (e.g. poverty), physical (e.g. disease), or natural disasters.

How the Qur'ān treats this distress was also discussed.

There are many types of calamities and afflictions, and it was shown how the Qur'ān offers three remedies. If a person uses all three of these remedies in combination, he will free himself from depression.

The first remedy is what the Qur'ān confirms and echoes repeatedly, which is that everything in this life is ordained. For example, death only comes at its appointed time and diseases only afflict by Allah's decree. The same goes for deformity or disfigurement, natural disasters, and being tested with wealth and poverty. All calamities are the result of Allah's plan.

Verses were cited in which Allah ﷻ confirms this truth, such as the verse:

﴿مَآ أَصَابَ مِن مُّصِيبَةٍ فِي ٱلْأَرْضِ وَلَا فِيٓ أَنفُسِكُمْ إِلَّا فِي كِتَٰبٍ مِّن قَبْلِ أَن نَّبْرَأَهَآ ۚ إِنَّ ذَٰلِكَ عَلَى ٱللَّهِ يَسِيرٌ ﴿٢٢﴾ لِّكَيْلَا تَأْسَوْا عَلَىٰ مَا فَاتَكُمْ وَلَا تَفْرَحُوا بِمَآ ءَاتَىٰكُمْ﴾

"Nothing occurs, either in the earth or in yourselves, without its being in a Book before We make it happen. That is something easy for Allah. That is so that you will not be grieved about the things that pass you by or exult about the things that come to you." [al-Ḥadīd 57:22-23]

If a person recognizes this truth, which is the first remedy, then he will not fall victim to the term 'if only'.[25]

'If only I had done so and so, if only I had followed up with the doctor on a regular basis and done the necessary tests, or if only I had been more cautious and done this and that, then such and such would not have happened.'

When the term 'if only' gets a hold of a person, it alone is one of the most dangerous diseases. Once he understands that nothing befalls him except by Allah's decree, he will understand that none of these 'if onlys' could have changed that decree, and therefore he will be untroubled.

This was the first remedy.

The second remedy is what Allah repeatedly confirms to us, which is the insignificance of this worldly life in which you live, with its sweetness and bitterness, and its good and bad. It is a passage to a destination. Man often falls victim to attaching more value and significance to this world than it is due. When he does that and is then afflicted with some calamity, he inevitably suffers from pain,

25 Ar. *law* (لـو) - used for unreal conditionals, e.g. 'If I had done such-and-such, such-and-such would not have happened'.

depression, and distress. However, when you listen repeatedly to Allah's words where He trivialises this world and clarifies for us that it is something insignificant and that what awaits us in the Hereafter, which is purer, longer lasting, and far superior, the factors of this distress ease and the causes of this depression melt away.

Look again at verses in which Allah trivialises for us the value of this world. For example:

﴿وَٱضْرِبْ لَهُم مَّثَلَ ٱلْحَيَوٰةِ ٱلدُّنْيَا كَمَآءٍ أَنزَلْنَٰهُ مِنَ ٱلسَّمَآءِ فَٱخْتَلَطَ
بِهِۦ نَبَاتُ ٱلْأَرْضِ فَأَصْبَحَ هَشِيمًا تَذْرُوهُ ٱلرِّيَٰحُ ۗ وَكَانَ ٱللَّهُ عَلَىٰ كُلِّ شَىْءٍ
مُّقْتَدِرًا ۝٤٥ ٱلْمَالُ وَٱلْبَنُونَ زِينَةُ ٱلْحَيَوٰةِ ٱلدُّنْيَا ۖ وَٱلْبَٰقِيَٰتُ ٱلصَّٰلِحَٰتُ
خَيْرٌ عِندَ رَبِّكَ ثَوَابًا وَخَيْرٌ أَمَلًا﴾

"Make a metaphor for them of the life of this world. It is like water which We send down from the sky and the plants of the earth combine with it but then become dry chaff scattered by the winds. Allah has absolute power over everything. Wealth and sons are the embellishment of the life of this world. But, in your Lord's sight, right actions which are lasting bring a better reward and are a better basis for hope." [al-Kahf 18:45-46]

You have read many similar verses. So, imagine if you satiate yourself with these verses after you believe that Allah is addressing you in them. This will be another remedy to ease the effects of this calamity.

The third remedy Allah informs us about is the system that He decreed for this worldly life. Allah brought us into existence on this earth according to the terms which He decreed, not according to the terms that we like. He also clarifies to us that the life that we live is not heaven or eternal bliss. Our life is a spectrum of good and evil. One day is profitable and the other is a loss. One day is for you and the other is against you. And no matter what you do to try to control this life, the system of this life will not differ from what Allah wills. Look at His statement:

﴿وَلَنَبْلُوَنَّكُم بِشَيْءٍ مِّنَ ٱلْخَوْفِ وَٱلْجُوعِ وَنَقْصٍ مِّنَ ٱلْأَمْوَٰلِ وَٱلْأَنفُسِ وَٱلثَّمَرَٰتِ﴾

"We will test you with a certain amount of fear and hunger and loss of wealth and life and fruits."
[al-Baqarah 2:155]

This statement is for all mankind, in every time and place. It is not exclusively for those who lived on the margins of history, were uneducated, and had no control over nature, while we, in this modern age, are able to free ourselves from all of this. No, this speech is for all generations until the Final Hour. There is no difference in this regard between a rich country and a poor country, nor is there a difference between a people who have mastered the natural sciences and controlled them completely and a people who are still in the darkness of ignorance. There is no difference. This applies to all of them. "We will test you with a certain amount of fear and hunger and loss of wealth and life and fruits."

Then, look at the cure:

﴿وَبَشِّرِ ٱلصَّٰبِرِينَ ۝١٥٥ ٱلَّذِينَ إِذَآ أَصَٰبَتْهُم مُّصِيبَةٌ قَالُوٓا۟ إِنَّا لِلَّهِ وَإِنَّآ إِلَيْهِ رَٰجِعُونَ ۝١٥٦ أُو۟لَٰٓئِكَ عَلَيْهِمْ صَلَوَٰتٌ مِّن رَّبِّهِمْ وَرَحْمَةٌ ۖ وَأُو۟لَٰٓئِكَ هُمُ ٱلْمُهْتَدُونَ﴾

"But give good news to the steadfast: Those who, when disaster strikes them, say, 'We belong to Allah and to Him we will return.' Those are the people who will have blessings and mercy from their Lord; they are the ones who are guided." [al-Baqarah 2:155-157]

When you have faith in Allah, you are aware of how this life works, you know the conditions upon which you were brought into existence, and then you listen to Allah's Words when He says: "Give good news to the steadfast: Those who, when disaster strikes them, say, 'We belong to Allah and to Him we will return.' Those are the people who will have blessings and mercy from their Lord; they are the ones who are guided"; at that moment, peace from these divine words enters your heart.

A calamity is undoubtedly a calamity and its pains are present and real. However, it does not cause you what is called depression or constant distress. You remain in a state of surrender to Allah and, moreover, you remain satisfied with the decree of Allah.

Combine these three remedies and watch how effective they are in getting rid of depression.

Having no Hope of Forgiveness

There is one more phenomenon left with regards to the third cause of depression, which shall now be explained in more detail.

There are many young people who indulge in all kinds of sin, disobey Allah at every opportunity, are utterly reckless, and then, one day, they reconcile with Allah and repent. Many of them, after repenting, still feel the impact of their past. They think that the sins they have committed are too big and treacherous for Allah to forgive them. The shadow and darkness of those sins still chase them wherever they go and no matter how hard they try to forget them. They constantly find themselves face to face with their dark and ugly past although at present they are reconciled with Allah.

Due to this state, they experience psychological anxiety, and if this anxiety continues, it transforms into distress and depression.

What is the cause of this depression?

Satanic whisperings haunt them and make them question the point of their repentance. It prompts them to relive and visualise their dirty past. 'Remember the sin you committed on that day and the atrocity you committed on such and such day. Have you forgotten all of this? Have you forgotten that this is all recorded against you? Your book of deeds is stained with everything you have committed!'

This whispering haunts them continuously. Who are the ones, mostly from the youth, that fall victim to such whisperings? It is those that have reconciled with Allah emotionally but are lacking in knowledge when it comes to religion, the Revealed Law, and the manner in which Allah deals with his slaves. Consequently, they imagine that Allah will not forgive them because they have committed too many sins. What is the remedy in the Qur'ān to free these people from these Satanic whisperings?

The remedy is in the verses in which Allah confirms repeatedly that He accepts repentance, He is merciful, and forgiving of all sins and the only thing a person needs to do is glance in the direction of his Lord and creator and make a benevolent return to Him via heartfelt words:

'O' Lord, I have returned to You so please accept me.'

Allah will say to them: 'Here I am. I have accepted you as you are.'

You can read the meaning of these words clearly in the Qur'ān. For example:

﴿قُلْ يَٰعِبَادِىَ ٱلَّذِينَ أَسْرَفُوا۟ عَلَىٰٓ أَنفُسِهِمْ لَا تَقْنَطُوا۟ مِن رَّحْمَةِ
ٱللَّهِ ۚ إِنَّ ٱللَّهَ يَغْفِرُ ٱلذُّنُوبَ جَمِيعًا ۚ إِنَّهُۥ هُوَ ٱلْغَفُورُ ٱلرَّحِيمُ﴾

"Say: 'My slaves, you who have transgressed against yourselves, do not despair of the mercy of Allah. Truly Allah forgives all wrong actions. He is the Ever-Forgiving, the Most Merciful.'" [az-Zumar 39:53]

The youth that have repented to Allah will not fall victim to this whispering unless they are far from His words and have not understood them. However, those who have read those words, there is no doubt that they have freed themselves from that whispering.

This meaning is repeated in a loving and attractive manner in the Qur'ān. Look, for example, at what Allah ﷻ says:

﴿وَٱلَّذِينَ إِذَا فَعَلُوا فَـٰحِشَةً أَوْ ظَلَمُوٓا أَنفُسَهُمْ ذَكَرُوا ٱللَّهَ فَٱسْتَغْفَرُوا لِذُنُوبِهِمْ وَمَن يَغْفِرُ ٱلذُّنُوبَ إِلَّا ٱللَّهُ وَلَمْ يُصِرُّوا عَلَىٰ مَا فَعَلُوا﴾

"Those who, when they act indecently or wrong themselves, remember Allah and ask forgiveness for their bad actions (and who can forgive bad actions except Allah?) and do not knowingly persist in what they were doing." [Āl ʿImrān 3:135]

Who can forgive sins except Allah? If Allah, the first to forgive and accept repentance, is not the one who forgives sins, then who does?

Forgiving is His standard practice and one of His attributes.

Let us look at the verses that precede the verses quoted above:

﴿وَسَارِعُوٓا إِلَىٰ مَغْفِرَةٍ مِّن رَّبِّكُمْ وَجَنَّةٍ عَرْضُهَا ٱلسَّمَـٰوَٰتُ وَٱلْأَرْض أُعِدَّتْ لِلْمُتَّقِينَ﴾

"Race each other to forgiveness from your Lord and a Garden as wide as the heavens and the earth, prepared for the people who have piety[26]." [Āl ʿImrān 3:133]

Allah describes those who have piety as:

﴿ٱلَّذِينَ يُنفِقُونَ فِي ٱلسَّرَّآءِ وَٱلضَّرَّآءِ وَٱلۡكَٰظِمِينَ ٱلۡغَيۡظَ وَٱلۡعَافِينَ عَنِ ٱلنَّاسِۗ وَٱللَّهُ يُحِبُّ ٱلۡمُحۡسِنِينَ ١٣٤ وَٱلَّذِينَ إِذَا فَعَلُواْ فَٰحِشَةً أَوۡ ظَلَمُوٓاْ أَنفُسَهُمۡ ذَكَرُواْ ٱللَّهَ فَٱسۡتَغۡفَرُواْ لِذُنُوبِهِمۡ وَمَن يَغۡفِرُ ٱلذُّنُوبَ إِلَّا ٱللَّهُ وَلَمۡ يُصِرُّواْ عَلَىٰ مَا فَعَلُواْ﴾

"Those who give in times of both ease and hardship, those who control their rage and pardon other people – Allah loves the good-doers – those who, when they act indecently or wrong themselves, remember Allah and ask forgiveness for their bad actions (and who can forgive bad actions except Allah?) and do not knowingly persist in what they were doing." [Āl ʿImrān 3:134-135]

"Those who, when they act indecently or wrong themselves" is also part of the description of those who have piety. They are not infallible. They are not above committing sins. However, when they do so, they "remember Allah and ask forgiveness for their bad actions", and " do not knowingly persist in what they were doing."

The slaves seek forgiveness for their sins and then comes the role of Allah ﷻ. He says: "and who can forgive bad actions except Allah?"

There are youth who filled their lives with sins, and we can even assume they were major sins, and then they returned to Allah and said:

26 Ar. *al-muttaqīn.*

'O' Lord, we have returned to You, so please accept our repentance.'

There is no doubt that Allah responds and says: 'Welcome My slaves, you have repented and I have forgiven you and accepted your repentance.'

It is then that this distress is removed. And in order for the sinners not to fall victim to the whispers of Shayṭān, the Prophet ﷺ confirmed this truth for them.

Look at this *ḥadīth qudsi:*[27]

It is on the authority of Anas ؓ who said, 'I heard the Messenger of Allah ﷺ saying, {Allah says, 'Son of Adam, as long as you call on Me and hope in Me, I will forgive whatever comes from you and I do not care. Son of Adam, even if your sins were to reach the clouds in the sky and then you were to seek My forgiveness, I would forgive you. Son of Adam, even if you were to come to Me with nearly the earth in wrong actions, and then you were to meet Me and not associate any partner with Me, I would bring you the same in forgiveness.'}[28]

After listening to these words, is it possible for depression to afflict a person who has repented to Allah and to be plagued with regret over his past sins? It is not possible if this young person studies and understands Allah's words and the words of His Messenger ﷺ. ʿUmar ibn al-Khaṭṭāb [29] ؓ reported that some prisoners were

---

27 i.e. a text in which the Messenger of Allah ﷺ quotes a statement from Allah and it is not from the Qurʾān. For further details, please see the commentary on 24th ḥadīth in *Al-Wāfī: A Thorough Commentary on the Forty Nawāwiyyah*, 206-207.

28 Related by at-Tirmidhī, who said that it is a good, authentic ḥadīth. This is the 42nd ḥadīth in *Al-Wāfī: A Thorough Commentary on the Forty Nawāwiyyah.*

29 He is the Commander of the Believers, ʿUmar ibn al-Khaṭṭāb al-Qurashī al-ʿAdawī, Abū Ḥafs, the second of the Rightly-Guided Caliphs. He was an ambassador for Quraysh in *al-Jāhiliyyah* and at the beginning of the Mission, he was firmly against the Muslims. Then, he embraced Islam and his Islam was an opening for them and a relief for them from distress. ʿAbdullah ibn Masʿūd said, 'We could not pray by the Kaʿbah until ʿUmar had

brought to Allah's Messenger ﷺ amongst whom was a woman who was searching for her child. When she found a child amongst the prisoners, she took hold of him, pressed him against her chest and fed it. Allah's Messenger ﷺ then said:

{Do you think this woman would ever throw her child in a fire?} We said: 'By Allah, she would never throw the child in a fire.' The Messenger of Allah ﷺ then said: {Allah is more merciful to His slave than this woman is to her child.}[30]

In this ḥadīth, the Arabic letter *lam* that precedes the word "Allah" in "Allah is more merciful to His slave than this woman is to her child" is for emphasis and is an oath. Thus, inform the youth that have reconciled with Allah after committing sins, obscenities, deviations, and all the wrongs you can imagine that the mercy of Allah ﷻ is greater and far outweighs your sins, and the light of divine forgiveness is much brighter than the darkness of your obscenities. Inform these brothers who have repented that if Allah ﷻ did not love them, He would not have drawn them near to Himself via repentance. Let the repentant know that one of the greatest proofs of Allah's love for him is that he turned to Allah with repentance and returned to Him.

When you are corrupt and completely immersed in sin, as much as you want and desire, and then suddenly you find yourself disgusted with these sins and yearning to repent and to return to

---

become Muslim'. His Islam was after forty men had become Muslim and eleven women, in the sixth year of the mission. He migrated openly, in front of Quraysh, and he partook in all the battles of the Messenger of Allah ﷺ. He was given the pledge of allegiance as the caliph after the death of Abū Bakr as-Ṣiddīq ؓ in the year 12 AH, based on a covenant from him. He was martyred in the year 23 AH after Abū Lu'lu' al-Majūsī stabbed him in his waist while he was performing the dawn prayer. He lived for three nights after the stabbing, may Allah the Exalted have mercy on him and be pleased with him. (*Al-Wāfī: A Thorough Commentary on the Forty Nawāwiyyah*, p.446)

30 Agreed upon (al-Bukhari and Muslim).

Allah, at that moment you must know that you are beloved to Allah, because if Allah did not love you, He would not have placed disgust for these sins in your heart and the yearning to repent to Him.

Knowing this, how can you allow Shayṭān a way into your heart to insert depression into it? How can you let him make you think that your sins are greater than Allah's forgiveness? Seek refuge in Allah from Shayṭān.

Allah ﷻ forgives all sins.

Look at another *ḥadīth qudsi*:

Abu Hurairah ﷺ reported that the Prophet ﷺ said: {Allah ﷻ said: 'A slave committed a sin and said: "O Allah, forgive my sin."' Allah then said: 'My slave committed a sin and then realised that he has a Lord who forgives sins and punishes sins.[31] He then committed a sin and said: "My Lord, forgive my sin."' Allah ﷻ said: 'My slave committed a sin and then realised that he has a Lord who forgives sins and punishes sins. He again committed a sin and said: "My Lord, forgive my sin."' Allah ﷻ then said: 'My slave has committed a sin and then realized that he has a Lord Who forgives sins and punishes sins. I have granted forgiveness to my slave. Let him do whatever he likes.[32]'}[33]

These words that the Messenger of Allah ﷺ narrated from his Lord indicate that Allah's forgiveness is greater than any sin, regardless of its magnitude, and that Allah's mercy towards His slaves is far greater than the mercy humans show one another. Those who strengthen their faith and repentance to Allah with knowledge, by approaching and contemplating Allah's Book,

31 i.e. if He wants.

32 i.e. as long as he continues to repent for his sins. See the 42nd ḥadīth in *Al-Wāfi: A Thorough Commentary on the Forty Nawāwiyyah*, section 8.

33 Agreed upon (al-Bukhārī and Muslim). Please see *Nuzhat al-Muttaqīn Sharḥ Riyāḍ as-Ṣāliḥīn* (Beirut: Muʾassasah ar-Risālah, 1407/1987), 1:383. This is Ḥadīth no. 432 in the Dār al-Minhāj edition of *Riyāḍ as-Ṣāliḥīn*, 190-191.

understanding its meanings as well as approaching the explanations of His Book in the ḥadīths of the Messenger of Allah ﷺ, can never be afflicted by depression.

In addition, have you asked yourself: why does Shayṭān afflict people with these whisperings? Why would Shayṭān make people worry about their sins? He is supposed to tempt man with sins. Why would Shayṭān warn man about the severity of his sins and tell him that they are too wicked to be forgiven? Why?

The answer:

Shayṭān wants people to feel that their repentance is pointless and therefore there is no need to tire themselves with righteous deeds and obedience. Why should you waste your time trying to get closer to Allah? Just go back to what you were doing before.

That is the deception that Shayṭān is aiming at, to place in the mind of the sinner that his repentance is worthless and that after all that he has committed, there is no hope of his attaining Allah's mercy. When this illusion takes root in someone's mind, an overwhelming depression afflicts him, as is seen with many of the youths that have repented to Allah. In the end, they flee from their depression by going back to their former way of life. They tell themselves, 'Since there is no hope or good in us, we may as well go back to what we used to do and try our luck in this worldly life with whatever time we have left'. And that is how Shayṭān celebrates based on this deception with which he fools man.

Nevertheless, the remedy for everything is knowledge. Learn what Allah communicates to you, listen to His advice, contemplate His speech to you, and then look at what the Messenger of Allah ﷺ says. Then Shayṭān will never be able to deceive you.

This was part of the third cause of depression that afflicts some, not all, of those that repent and then ruminate their sinful past. The Messenger of Allah ﷺ taught us that if we repent to Allah, we need to place our past days behind us, forget all of them, and imagine that we are reborn.

May Allah ﷻ bless us with a good return to His Book and the Sunnah of His Messenger ﷺ.

Chapter Six
The Fourth Cause: The Fear of Death

The first three causes of depression have been discussed. Two remain.

The fourth cause is the fear of death, which many people have. They imagine death to be some unknown, dreadful spectre that is slowly creeping towards them. This imagination puts anxiety and unrest in the hearts of many people, which then leads their souls into a state of depression.

Secular, materialistic societies are overflowing with those who have been afflicted with depression because of this cause. In Islamic societies, this cause may appear to be non-existent, but it exists. If you were to compare, however, between Islamic societies and secular, materialistic societies, you would find a huge difference.

This is because Muslim societies live under the shade of knowing Allah. They are under the shade of being familiar and intimate with Allah. They are under the shade of knowing the reality of life and death, because they pay attention and listen to what Allah ﷻ says.

As you know, however, the ripples of those secular, materialistic illnesses have inevitably reached Muslim countries as well. The contagions of depression and anxiety have penetrated our societies. Now, we too have people who are constantly depressed because of this reason.

The reason is that a person like this, whenever he remembers death or is reminded of death, it is as if he remembers something unknown. He is not able to grasp its reality. He views death the way one of us would view a spectre coming over the horizon, a spectre coming from far away. He does not know what it is; yet slowly but surely, this spectre creeps closer and closer to him. Every time it gets closer, it becomes more imposing, but he does not know what this spectre is, or what it wants to do with him.

This person inevitably becomes a victim of this fear, and falls into depression and anxiety.

There are many people for whom death is a hidden, unknown, spectre. They do not know anything about its reality.

So what is the treatment?

The treatment, before everything else, is for us to learn. Before anything else, the Qurʾān has charged us with knowledge. It has charged us not to take one step in the field of creed unless it is based on knowledge. The second step must be based on knowledge. The third step, the fourth, and so on, must be based on knowledge.

This, therefore, calls on us to become familiar with the reality of death: what is death?

The scholars before us researched this topic, in response to Allah's ﷻ command. One should pay attention and listen to these words in order to become comfortable with death, instead of having an aversion to it.

If you grasp the reality that will be described below, you will be comfortable with it instead of having an aversion to it - if your conduct in this life is conduct that pleases Allah ﷻ.

Whether he is alive and walking on this earth or lying down dead inside of it, man is always binary in his constitution. He comprises two things: a body and a spirit. However, when man is alive, his spirit is imprisoned within his body. That is, the spirit is subordinate to the body. The spirit is confined to this bodily enclosure. The spirit, therefore, can only move with the body's movement; right, left, forward, backward, and so forth.

When a person dies, he remains binary in his constitution, but the situation is inverted. The body becomes subordinate to the spirit, after the spirit had been subordinate to the body. The spirit is thus set free, to go wherever it wants. When the spirit is not confined to this bodily enclosure, nothing obstructs its way, nothing hinders it; nothing prevents the spirit going wherever it wants to. This is if the person's life has a good end.

As for the person who is ignorant of Allah, who displays arrogance towards Allah; when this person dies, his spirit is imprisoned in what Allah has called *sijjīn*.[34] As a result of this, the body is afflicted with a permanent tribulation and a painful punishment. The spirit moves from the prison of the body that it was into another prison called *sijjīn*, until that day on which everyone is resurrected.

Therefore, the spirit always exists and is always present. Its connection to the body continues. Again, while a person is alive, his spirit is imprisoned in his body. When he dies, his body is imprisoned by his spirit.

34 See Surat al-Muṭaffifīn 83:17.

If a person's life ends with a good end, and he devotes himself to Allah after repenting to Him, his spirit is set free. It moves of its own accord; it can go east, it can go west, it can go wherever it wants.

And as the Messenger of Allah ﷺ has informed us, its connection to this body remains, regardless of whether it is swallowed by a whale, or buried in the earth like everyone else, or if anything else happens to it. The spirit's connection to the body continues and it is complete, just like the sun's connection to the earth. The sun is separate from the earth in its mass, but it is connected to the earth by way of its rays. The sun appears in the east, it appears in the west; wherever it is, its rays fall on the earth. This is exactly how the spirit is. Wherever the spirit goes, its rays emanate and reach this body. When Allah ﷻ seals someone's life with a good end, the spirit's felicity is reflected in the body. The bliss and delights that this spirit enjoys are also reflected in the body, even though, when you look at this body, it appears motionless. It appears to be devoid of the spirit, because the spirit is no longer inside of it. This is the case even if you can see that the body has broken down, or decomposed, and has disintegrated into tiny pieces. This has no bearing on the reality that we are describing. The spirit's rays reach this body.

What is being stated here is rooted in knowledge. You need to understand that death does not mean non-existence. Death is not like a candle lighting a room that is then blown out. No. Man remains binary in his constitution, composed of both a body and a spirit. Is there any evidence for this in Allah's ﷻ Speech that when a person dies, he remains binary in his constitution? That his spirit remains? That he continues to feel his spirit? Look at the story of the believer who came running from the far side of the city, who advised his brethren and the people of his land to pay attention and listen to the Messengers and Prophets who had been sent to them, and not be haughty towards them, and to believe in them, Allah ﷻ says:

﴿وَجَآءَ مِنْ أَقْصَا ٱلْمَدِينَةِ رَجُلٌ يَسْعَىٰ قَالَ يَٰقَوْمِ ٱتَّبِعُوا۟ ٱلْمُرْسَلِينَ
٢٠ ٱتَّبِعُوا۟ مَن لَّا يَسْـَٔلُكُمْ أَجْرًا وَهُم مُّهْتَدُونَ ٢١ وَمَا لِىَ لَآ أَعْبُدُ
ٱلَّذِى فَطَرَنِى وَإِلَيْهِ تُرْجَعُونَ ٢٢ ءَأَتَّخِذُ مِن دُونِهِۦٓ ءَالِهَةً إِن يُرِدْنِ
ٱلرَّحْمَٰنُ بِضُرٍّ لَّا تُغْنِ عَنِّى شَفَٰعَتُهُمْ شَيْـًٔا وَلَا يُنقِذُونِ ٢٣ إِنِّىٓ إِذًا
لَّفِى ضَلَٰلٍ مُّبِينٍ﴾

"A man came running from the far side of the city, saying, 'My people! Follow the Messengers! Follow those who do not ask you for any wage and who have received guidance. Why indeed should I not worship Him Who brought me into existence, Him to Whom you will be returned? Am I to take as gods instead of Him those whose intercession, if the All-Merciful desires harm for me, will not help me at all and cannot save me? In that case I would be clearly misguided'." [Yā Sīn 36:20-24]

This man was then killed. Look at what Allah says about him after that:

﴿قِيلَ ٱدْخُلِ ٱلْجَنَّةَ ۖ قَالَ يَٰلَيْتَ قَوْمِى يَعْلَمُونَ ٢٦ بِمَا غَفَرَ لِى رَبِّى
وَجَعَلَنِى مِنَ ٱلْمُكْرَمِينَ﴾

"He was told: 'Enter the Garden!' He said: 'If my people only knew how my Lord has forgiven me and placed me among the honoured ones.'" [Yā Sīn 36:26-27]

This is what death is. **"He was told: 'Enter the Garden!'"** When was this said to him? On the Day of Standing?[35] No. On the Day of Standing, everyone is gathered together, and therefore there is no need to say 'if my people only knew'. On the Day of Standing, they will know.

Rather, these words were said to him immediately after death. The spirit heard these words, and the body enjoyed the spirit's felicity, as mentioned before.

﴿وَتِلْكَ ٱلْجَنَّةُ ٱلَّتِىٓ أُورِثْتُمُوهَا بِمَا كُنتُمْ تَعْمَلُونَ﴾

"He was told: 'Enter the Garden!'" "That is the Garden that you will inherit..." [az-Zukhruf 43:72]

What did he then say? **"He said: 'If my people only knew how my Lord has forgiven me and placed me among the honoured ones'."**

These are Allah's ﷻ words and Allah is the Creator of both life and death. These words show that death means to move from one type of life to another type of life, a life that is called the *barzakh.*[36] Understand this properly, and you will be certain of it when you move to it. May Allah make our move to it like the move of this believer from the Children of Israel, this person who gave sincere advice to his brethren, gave sincere advice to his nation, and they did not heed his advice. Then, when he moved to Allah's magnanimity, Allah honoured him with this felicity.

Look at Allah's ﷻ words when He addresses us:

﴿وَلَئِن مُّتُّمْ أَوْ قُتِلْتُمْ لَإِلَى ٱللَّهِ تُحْشَرُونَ﴾

35 Ar. *yawm al-qiyāmah.*

36 See Sūrat al-Muʾminūn 23:100.

"If you die or you are killed, it is to Allah that you will be gathered." [Āl ʿImrān 3:158]

Death does not mean non-existence. Death is a person's drawing nearer to Allah, a person's moving to Allah's ﷻ magnanimity. The realities that a person sees in his *barzakh* life, after his move, via the door of death, are far more sublime, far more sublime, than the realities that we see today while we are confined to this bodily enclosure.

Then, look at other verses in which Allah talks about those who reject faith and act haughtily when the angels of death come to them to take their spirits, and how the angels say to them:

﴿أَخْرِجُوٓا۟ أَنفُسَكُمُ ۖ ٱلْيَوْمَ تُجْزَوْنَ عَذَابَ ٱلْهُونِ بِمَا كُنتُمْ تَقُولُونَ عَلَى ٱللَّهِ غَيْرَ ٱلْحَقِّ ...﴾

"Disgorge yourselves! Today you will be repaid with the punishment of humiliation for saying other than the truth about Allah..." [al-Anʿām 6:93]

Today, i.e. not the Day of Standing.

Therefore, in this life, the spirit is there, and man is binary of constitution. In this life, our spirit is imprisoned within this bodily enclosure. After death, the body is imprisoned by the spirit. The spirit roams the horizons - if it had a good end.

What is being described here is based on knowledge. All Muslim scholars have said this. No one is ignorant of this except someone who is deviating from knowledge *in the name* of knowledge.[37]

Your attention should then be drawn to a phenomenon that just about everyone knows but does not know the wisdom behind it.

37 Or in the name of science, for that matter.

Think of someone sitting in his bedroom, and he sits there for several hours. Then he sleeps in that same room from the evening through to the morning. Then he finds that he desperately needs to go out onto the balcony, and to be invigorated by some fresh air.

He goes out onto the balcony - and you can imagine that this balcony has a great view, overlooking vast horizons - how does he feel at this moment? When he looks out from this balcony, over these vast horizons that stretch out as far as the eye can see, he feels a happiness that is unlike any other. He feels a comfort and ease that is unlike any other.

It would be very different if this balcony did not overlook a vast, beautiful view. If this balcony only offered a view of another building's wall, a hundred metres away, for example, and maybe in this space there were gardens with flowers and aromatic fragrances, he would not find that same bliss and happiness at all, the same happiness he would find if the balcony were overlooking a wide, open, space, stretching as far as the eye can see, even if this space were bare and empty.

Everyone feels this. Why does a person feel that there is something fluttering within him when he exits his room, even though all the means of comfort are there and available? Why does he have these feelings? Why does he feel this elation when he is able to look over a vast space, stretching as far as the eye can see? Why?

It is because the spirit is imprisoned within this enclosure. When the spirit is able to look over the vastness of this world, it becomes excited. This is because the spirit's nature is to be set free. Its nature is not to be confined within this body. In this state, the spirit uses the body's window – these two eyes – and it looks over this space, and it is as if it says: 'When will I be set free? When will I be able to traverse this world in a split second, from one end to the other, from one horizon to the other? When will I be granted this?'

You might not feel the spirit's longing and its language, but this is what the spirit says. This is how it talks.

When the spirit leaves the prison of this body, the exit is happy, the exit that is preceded by a good end. It is like a wedding for the spirit.

This meaning is overflowing in Allah's Book ﷻ.

﴿وَلَئِن مُّتُّمْ أَوْ قُتِلْتُمْ لَإِلَى ٱللَّهِ تُحْشَرُونَ﴾

"If you die or you are killed, it is to Allah that you will be gathered." [Āl ʿImrān 3:158]

Look at this person who was killed. He had given his people sincere advice and they did not accept it. What did he say immediately after he was killed?

﴿قِيلَ ٱدْخُلِ ٱلْجَنَّةَ ۖ قَالَ يَـٰلَيْتَ قَوْمِى يَعْلَمُونَ ۝٢٦ بِمَا غَفَرَ لِى رَبِّى وَجَعَلَنِى مِنَ ٱلْمُكْرَمِينَ﴾

"He was told: 'Enter the Garden!' He said: 'If my people only knew how my Lord has forgiven me and placed me among the honoured ones.'" [Yā Sīn 36:26-27]

You must allow yourself to be sated by this – and Allah's Book always talks to us about it and clarifies it for us. Notice Allah has attached our actions to rewards. He ﷻ says:

﴿فَٱسْتَجَابَ لَهُمْ رَبُّهُمْ أَنِّى لَآ أُضِيعُ عَمَلَ عَـٰمِلٍ مِّنكُم مِّن ذَكَرٍ أَوْ أُنثَىٰ﴾

"Their Lord responds to them: 'I will not let the deeds of any doer among you go to waste, male or female'." [Āl ʿImrān 3:195]

It is not possible; all of your deeds are recorded. It is as if Allah is saying, 'I shall give you your rewards, all of you, and I shall not distinguish between males and females.'

Everyone asks: when will this happen, this day of reward? Allah connects the reward to death. Why? It is so that we feel familiar and comfortable with death, which is the path that leads to that reward. He ﷻ says:

﴿كُلُّ نَفْسٍ ذَآئِقَةُ ٱلْمَوْتِ ۗ وَإِنَّمَا تُوَفَّوْنَ أُجُورَكُمْ يَوْمَ ٱلْقِيَـٰمَةِ ۖ فَمَن زُحْزِحَ عَنِ ٱلنَّارِ وَأُدْخِلَ ٱلْجَنَّةَ فَقَدْ فَازَ ۗ وَمَا ٱلْحَيَوٰةُ ٱلدُّنْيَآ إِلَّا مَتَـٰعُ ٱلْغُرُورِ﴾

"Every soul will taste death. You will be paid your wages in full on the Day of Standing. Anyone who is distanced from the Fire and admitted to Paradise has triumphed. The life of this world is just the enjoyment of delusion."
[Āl ʿImrān 3:185]

You will be paid your wages in full on the Day of Standing. Therefore, if you know that death means drawing nearer to reward, i.e. it will lead you to reward, as Allah ﷻ has said, then how can you know Allah, pay attention to and listen to His words, and then be averse to death? How?

This is the remedy, but use the remedy! If we apply the remedy, all of us will become like Bilāl al-Ḥabashī.[38] What do we know about Bilal al-Ḥabashī? When he was lying on his deathbed and

38 He is Bilāl ibn Rabāh al-Ḥabashī ؓ the one who called to the prayer (*muʿadhdhin*). He was also known as Bilāl ibn Ḥamāmah, which was his mother's name. Abū Bakr as-Ṣiddīq ؓ bought him from the idol-worshippers when they were torturing him for professing *tawḥīd* and set him free. He then accompanied the Prophet ﷺ and gave the call to prayer for him, and witnessed all of the battles with him. When he arrived in al-Madīnah, the Prophet ﷺ made him and Abū ʿUbaydah ibn al-Jarrāḥ brothers. After the Prophet's ﷺ death, he fought in more battles and died in Shām. Al-Bukhārī says that he died in Shām

his relatives were all around him, he heard one of them say: 'What agony!' Bilal immediately opened his eyes and said: 'Rather, what joy! Tomorrow, we shall meet our beloveds: Muḥammad and his Companions!'

All of us will be like Bilal. All of us. But you must know what death is, and grasp its reality, and then place between yourself and death a path, a path that is paved with obedience. Place between yourself and death a path that is paved with sincere slavehood to Allah, a path that is paved with repentance to Allah ﷻ.

That is when death will not be seen as some dreadful spectre. You will find that everything that was dreadful about this spectre has dissolved, and that it is actually a key to Paradise, a key to bliss, a key to achieving nearness to Allah.

This is what will free people from this type of depression.

If you still feel that the spectre of death makes you feel afraid and estranged, makes you feel sad and grieved, turn to Allah's Book, and contemplate what Allah says about death: how He describes and defines the reality of death, and what comes after death. It is also advisable to turn to the Messenger of Allah ﷺ and to listen to what he says about death: what the final outcome is for the person who dies and how Allah shows him his seat in Paradise, and he never stops feeling abundant joy every time he sees this seat that Allah ﷻ, has prepared for him.

in the time of ʿUmar. Abū Bukayr says that he died in the plague of ʿAmwās. ʿAmr ibn ʿAlī says that he died in the year 20 AH. See *Al-Iṣābah fī Tamyīz as-Ṣaḥābah* by Imam ibn Ḥajar al-ʿAsqalānī (Beirut: Dār al-Kutub al-ʿIlmiyyah, 1415/1995), 1:455-456. One can also read his biography on the Naseem al-Sham website: https://www.naseemalsham.com/subjects/view/14391.

Chapter Seven

The Fifth Cause:

The Inability To Achieve Personal Ambitions

The fifth cause of depression afflicts those people who feel unable to reach their goals, aspirations, and dreams that they were attached to, dreamt of, and always envisioned in their imagination and were always thinking about. Then suddenly, they find they are unable to realise those dreams. They are unable to achieve those aspirations for themselves. There are many that fall into a depression unlike no other, and they stay depressed because they never achieved the dreams and aspirations that they held for so long and were so diligently working towards.

This fifth cause afflicts different types of people including those who aspire to health without disease, wealth without poverty, and unwavering strength that is not overcome by any state of weakness. Those that aspire to whims, pleasures, delights, and desires that do not diminish or withdraw. As you have also come to know, this worldly life does not provide them with all these wishes exactly as they dreamt. Bearing in mind that these people are deeply attached to their goals and dreams, when they find that these thoughts will not be realised as they wanted and imagined, they clash with a reality that contradicts their dreams. Consequently, they fall into a state of worry and anguish that has no end or outlet.

It should not surprise you that those who fall victim to this type of depression are the same people to whom all the doors of pleasures, desires, and whims are open. They have thus immersed themselves in all kinds of gratification and mastered how to do so. However, they eventually crash into a dangerous and stubborn barrier.

What is this barrier?

It is one of the universal laws of this world that we live in.

And what is this law?

The law is that these pleasures and delights have a limit, after which man can go no further. Thus, no matter how much you try to creatively diversify enjoyment and amusement through money, youthfulness, luxuries, and desires, you will move from one form of pleasure to another until you will find yourself in front of a barrier that you cannot breach. Man has a tendency to become bored. He practises a form of pleasure for days or months and then he becomes bored. He uses creativity to transcend to another form of pleasure but then, after a while, he finds that form boring as well. Again, he creatively finds ways to transcend to a third form of pleasure but again tires of it after some time. Finally, he runs out of pleasures and he finds himself in front of a barrier that he cannot transcend. Then he looks with disgust at all the pleasures and delights, which he is now sick and tired of. He tries desperately to transcend creatively once again to new pleasures but he cannot. It is then that an unparalleled feeling of depression overwhelms him.

Were you aware of this truth? The secular, materialistic world is the first to fall victim to this type of depression. When a man arrives at this impenetrable barrier, after consuming all the means to amuse and entertain himself, he tries to be creative and amuse himself through imagination and dreams. How? He does this by resorting to substance abuse, such as drugs and alcohol and escaping from rationality to irrationality in order to imagine that he is melting into a vast world of pleasures without end. He then finds that the outcome of this cure is worse than the situation that he was in to begin with.

This reality is one example of the fifth cause of depression, in which man aspires and dreams of various pleasures. However, he manoeuvres within a circle of limited cosmic abilities that he cannot surpass. The laws of the universe are limited and so are the laws of pleasure, which he cannot breach and as a result, he is burdened with trepidation.

What do you make of those who aspire to a life of continuous good health but then fall into the path of disease, or those who build themselves a perfect marital home in their imagination and then it never becomes a reality? What about those who imagine that they are young, attractive, and beautiful but then realise that they are not?

The latter example is what afflicted the "father" of existentialism, Søren Kierkegaard.

Let us take a brief look at existentialist philosophy. This philosophy instructs its followers to direct their lives towards the utmost degree of pleasure, to plan to reach the highest degree of delight and to focus on a breathless pursuit of unblemished happiness. This is what existentialism places in the minds of its followers. So, when existentialists go through life trying to achieve this dream of untainted happiness and pure pleasures, they are shocked that the world is not so, that the pleasures of this world are limited, its troubles are many, its inconveniences and setbacks are constant, and that man is weak and limited and thus cannot live up to his ambitions and dreams. Consequently, the fantastic, glittery dreams that dominated their thoughts clash with the reality that the world imposes on them. When this is the case, as they themselves claim, feelings of sadness, distress, anxiety, despair, and failure overwhelm them.

How can they escape this philosophy? They do so by conceding to these things, that man is destined for anxiety, despair, and failure and he needs to ruminate his misery with patience and steadfastness and understand that this misery is his inevitable fate. Additionally, according to them, man must venture to reach his goals and if he does not reach them, he must accept that that is the nature of man and this life, and he needs to sit and ruminate his pains.

That was the summary of existentialist philosophy, in which they follow the example of their "father" and their great thinker, Søren Kierkegaard. When you look at the life of this man, you feel great pity for him. He would dream of infatuating people with his handsome appearance but people thought he was strange-looking. He fell in love with a girl and dreamed of her reciprocating that love and then building his happiness on that, but he failed. Additionally, he found that death was snatching his family members one after the other and feared that he was next in line. Wherever he looked, he found things that would cause him depression and when he looked to the future, he only saw the shadow of his death. As a result, he felt suffocated because everywhere he looked, the factors of depression surrounded him and he could not achieve in his lifetime what he dreamt of and aspired to. Kierkegaard went on to philosophise his misery and write it down. Many people believed it to be a scientific philosophy and that everyone needed to be clones of Søren Kierkegaard, to suffer the same miseries and feel the same depression as he did even if they did not go through the same experiences.

The key here is that existentialist philosophy is the result of a clash between a person's dreams and the worldly reality that denies him those dreams. The truth is that it is man who needs to align himself with the system of this world decreed by Allah ﷻ.

People who attach too much importance to their dreams are susceptible to this form of depression.

That was the illness. Now for the cure.

The cure here encompasses the sum of all the cures that were discussed in the previous chapters. First, this person needs to deal with the cures that were discussed by starting from a necessary foundation, which is the belief in Allah ﷻ, the Creator of this universe. This is the foundation for the remedies that he needs to implement. As for someone who is not a believer in Allah ﷻ, they must expect this depression to afflict them from any direction it wishes. This person is like a young sheep that has come out of its shelter and roams the vast fields where wild beasts are. The young sheep will inevitably be preyed upon by one of the beasts because it has left its safe shelter where it was.

Similarly, man's shelter from these types of depression resides in the genuine belief in Allah ﷻ and the trust in His wisdom and mercy. If this belief is not there then exposure to depression is continuous and there is no remedy. However, if you genuinely believe in Allah, and trust that He is All-Wise, i.e. He puts everything in its rightful place, and all-Merciful, i.e. although it might seem that He is being hard on you in certain matters, you trust that He is more merciful to you than you are to yourself, you will always live under the shade of Allah's words:

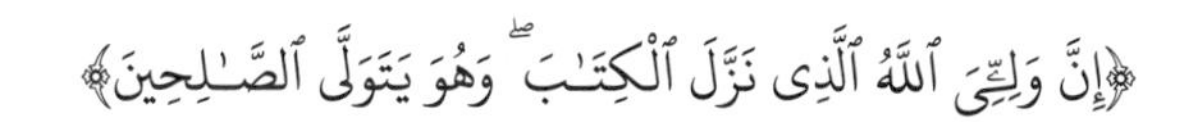

"My Protector is Allah who sent down the Book. He takes care of the righteous." [al-ʾAʿrāf 7:196]

The Qurʾān teaches us to repeat these words to ourselves. If we firmly believe this then the necessary foundation is there for the remedies that will be discussed. What is the cure after this? The cure is something you must not underestimate. It is a word repeated many times, and you might underestimate it. Its meaning, however, is an unprecedented antidote for this illness that is being discussed.

What is this word?

It is a lot of *dhikr*, i.e. remembrance of Allah ﷻ.

Some people underrate the word *dhikr* because they think *dhikr* is something traditional. When they hear the word *dhikr*, perhaps they imagine people gathering, moving their heads, jumping around, holding prayer beads in their hands, repeating the word "Allah" over and over again, and getting over-excited. Maybe this is what they imagine when they hear the word *dhikr*. This visualisation and connotation are incorrect. ***Dhikr* of Allah means to remember Allah always, in all situations that you come across in life.** Remembering Allah after believing in Him is an unprecedented medication. It melts away all the factors of depression, especially depression that overwhelms a person due to this fifth cause.

What is the evidence for this?

Listen to the words of Allah ﷻ, Whom we believe in and trust is All-Wise and Merciful, where He describes those that "remember":

﴿ٱلَّذِينَ ءَامَنُوا وَتَطْمَئِنُّ قُلُوبُهُم بِذِكْرِ ٱللَّهِ ۗ أَلَا بِذِكْرِ ٱللَّهِ تَطْمَئِنُّ ٱلْقُلُوبُ﴾

"Those who have believed and whose hearts find peace in the remembrance of Allah. Only in the remembrance of Allah can the heart find peace." [ar-Ra'd 13:28]

Notice the word "only".[39] In other words, understand the importance of what We are about to say. "Only in the remembrance of Allah can the heart find peace". This is the medicine! And it's a medicine declared by the words of Allah ﷻ. The source of depression is the heart.

What can bring you back to the shelter of tranquillity? What can make peace reside in your heart after you have believed in Allah? The answer is lots of *dhikr*. It is not necessary that this be a word that the tongue always repeats while a person is walking, sitting, before sleeping, and so on. Rather, you should remember Allah during the occasions that come your way, and the occasions that remind us of Allah are plenty. Whoever remembers Allah ﷻ abundantly, day after day, Allah removes any feelings of depression that he may have in his heart and replaces them with security, tranquillity, and joy. Don't ask how! There is no material cause. Rather, it is a secret Allah places in your heart.

When you continuously remember Allah, His wisdom, His mercy, His blessings, His favours, His creative originality, and His power, this remembrance pushes you to implore Allah and say: 'O Lord, I seek refuge in You from the situation I am in. O Lord, give my heart comfort and solace, ease my affairs, and remove this depression from my soul.' This remembrance leads you to always supplicate and beseech Allah and then you will find that the darkness of this monster within you dissipates and leaves you and is replaced by the light of contentment, tranquillity, and joy. Those who have tried know this truth.

There is practical evidence of this. There are many saints,[40] who enjoy an elevated degree of faith that exceeds that of the common people. However, they do not possess the kind of happiness that many people dream of for themselves. They do not have great riches, perfect health, or abundant wealth. Their joy and pleasure

39 Ar. *innamā*.
40 Ar. *walī*, pl. *awliyā*ʾ.

are not because of any material situation surrounding them, and yet, they are the epitome of happiness and pleasure. Their pleasure stems from within them and is reflected on their faces. It does not come to them from an external source. One of these saints, Ibrahim Ibn Adham ﷺ,[41] once said: 'If kings knew what we had, i.e. of happiness, joy, and pleasure, they would fight us for it with swords.' This was true of Ibrahim Ibn Adham ﷺ.

There are those who might be surprised at those words. They might look at Ibn Adham and see that he did not possess much wealth, a nice house, or any signs of a pleasurable marital life that he was immersed in. He did not possess any of those apparent things that make people happy. Thus, they might think to themselves: 'Why would kings fight you for this state when most likely they would flee from it?' Yes, kings would flee from his apparent outward state, but they do not know his inward state. Ibrahim Ibn Adham ﷺ is speaking about his heart and the pleasure that is fluttering inside of him, the pleasure that those who are with Allah feel after believing in Him through continuous remembrance and observance. Allah creates an unexplainable condition of happiness inside of them. Neither the kings nor those who have access to all the pleasures of the world feel this pleasure at all.

The reason for this has already been explained. There is a big difference between gathering the factors of pleasure from all around you and attaching them to your heart and when the source of pleasure stems from within your heart itself. In the former scenario, perhaps they enter your heart and perhaps they do not.

41 d.162/778. He is Abū Isḥāq Ibrāhīm ibn Adham ibn Mansūr Al-Balkhī, one of the grand Imams of the third age. He travelled to Makkah, Syria, Jordan, Lebanon and Palestine, sitting with noble scholars and Imams such as Sufyan ath-Thawrī and Al-Fuḍayl ibn ʿIyāḍ. Those in his time knew him to be a tireless preacher and constant in his worship. See *Tahdhīb al-Kamāl* by Imam Jamāl ad-Dīn al-Mizzī (Beirut: Muʾassasah ar-Risālah, 1402/1982), 2: 27-39.

For example, a man obtains money, pleasures, achieves his desires, has a luxurious house, and all the means of fun and entertainment are at his disposal. However, when he looks at his heart, he finds it distressed and sad. On the other hand, when Allah puts joy in your heart out of nowhere, this is the greatest spectacle. If those kings had been able to see the inside of Ibn Adham's heart, to see the state of his enjoyment and ecstasy, they certainly would have tried everything possible to transfer that state into their own hearts, even if they had to fight Ibn Adham and people like him for it. This is a fact.

When you look at slaves of Allah like Ibrahim Ibn Adham ﷺ, you find that the radiance of happiness always glows from their appearance and their faces. They do not know the meaning of sadness because for them, there is no connection between happiness and the reality of this world. The reality of the world moves in one direction while their feelings come from another direction. Their feelings come from above while this worldly life takes a separate path that Allah wills for it. Therefore, you know the truth of Allah's ﷻ words: **"Those who have believed and whose hearts find peace in the remembrance of Allah. Only in the remembrance of Allah can the heart find peace."** [ar-Raʿd 13:28]

Then there is the inverse of this statement. When a person has gone astray from Allah and is heedless of Him, and he roams the world looking to satisfy his whims, desires, and pleasures, and he builds - as much as he can - the means to achieve his dreams but he is oblivious of Allah, of the fact that everything is in His hands and that he is roaming in His kingdom; this person is exposed to a different verdict from Allah.

What is this verdict?

It is the verdict in which Allah ﷻ declares:

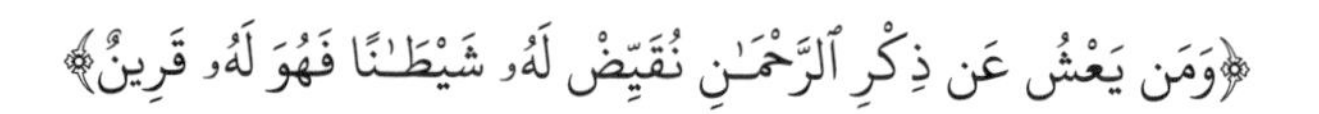

"If someone shuts his eyes to the remembrance of the All-Merciful, We assign him a shaytan who becomes his bosom friend." [az-Zukhruf 43:36]

This means that for the person who neglects and turns away from the remembrance of the All-Merciful, Allah appoints a shaytan for him who becomes his companion. This shaytan constantly instils depression in him and makes things seem graver than they really are. He also puts him in a state of disaffection and estrangement, even from himself.

Additionally, notice these words, "If someone shuts his eyes to the remembrance of the All-Merciful". Here Allah intentionally calls Himself the "All-Merciful". Why? It is to clarify for us that whoever remembers Allah ﷻ, Allah pledges and blesses him with mercy. Allah takes care of his affairs for him and removes the sources of depression. Here Allah calls himself a name that shows the treatment and remedy for the person who is afflicted with depression. It is as if he is telling you: 'Hey you! Here is the All-Merciful in front of you, your healer who provides you with what you need.' The key to your heart is in His hands. In one moment, He can transform your heart from one that is eaten up with depression into a heart that is fluttering with joy.

Allah ﷻ is in front of you; He is your healer and your mercy. So why do you turn away from His remembrance?

For that reason, Allah did not say: 'If someone shuts his eyes to the remembrance of Allah'. Perhaps someone will say: 'How can Allah benefit me in this case?' Instead, He said "All-Merciful", so that you know the reason why He is inviting you to His remembrance. Remember Him, knock on His door, treat your illness at

His hands, seek refuge in Him for the cure, and remember Him constantly - after believing that He is Allah, the All-Wise, the All-Merciful. You will find this meaning that Allah has clarified for us.

And you can see the same meaning in the covenant that Allah committed Himself to when He said:

﴿ٱلَّذِينَ ءَامَنُوا وَلَمْ يَلْبِسُوٓا إِيمَـٰنَهُم بِظُلْمٍ أُولَـٰٓئِكَ لَهُمُ ٱلْأَمْنُ وَهُم مُّهْتَدُونَ﴾

"Those who have believed and do not mix up their belief with any wrongdoing, they are the ones who are safe; it is they who are guided." [al-An'ām 6:82]

Allah is referring to those whose faith is not based on mere imitation. There are many people who believe with their mouths but do not carry in their hearts any of the responsibilities of this faith. Therefore, Allah is talking about those who genuinely believe, and He indicated this genuine belief by saying: "Those who have believed and do not mix up their belief with any wrongdoing". It is they and no one else "who are safe; it is they who are guided."

Where do safety and security stem from? From the heart. Safety does not come from your surroundings; it comes from your heart. If Allah ﷻ does not make you feel safe and tranquil, know that even if He were to place you in a shaded garden, you would still feel wretched and estranged. You can be sure of this. However, when you are a believer in Allah ﷻ and you have followed your faith with abundant remembrance of Allah and being aware of Him, this will lead you to the sanctum of supplication and prayer, and you will always be seeking refuge in Allah ﷻ, asking Him to give your heart comfort and solace, and to grant you relief from depression. When you remain consistent in this state, Allah ﷻ will then grant you safety and tranquillity from where you do not know or even expect. This is a fact that we must all understand.

There are people who claim that they believe in Allah and trust in His wisdom and mercy and nevertheless, depression in its various forms frequently finds its way into their feelings and into their hearts. The dreams that these people pursue are plenty and despite their faith in Allah, they suffer from depression when those dreams do not come true. The issue here is the faith that is based on mere imitation, whereas the faith that the verse refers to is the kind that leads a person to the continuous remembrance of Allah.

Are you consistent with your remembrance of Allah? When you sit at your dinner table, does the food remind you of Allah? When you retire to your bed, do you remember Allah before you fall asleep? When you wake up and you feel alert and energetic after such a deep slumber, do you remember Allah ﷻ?

You can take this further. Are you grateful to Allah after relieving yourself? When you are thirsty and you drink fresh cold water, does this remind you of Allah? When you see the various fruits in front of you to choose from at the fruit stand, do their colours, aromas, tastes, shapes, and creative originality remind you of Allah ﷻ?

By Allah, if all of this reminds you of Allah, this will lead you to trust in Him, believe in His mercy, and then you will extend your hand in supplication to Him. Those who are depressed will then see their depression vanish.

Chapter Eight

The Fifth Cause:

The Inability To Achieve Personal Ambitions (Continued)

Cognitive-Behavioural Therapy: Part One

As you know, the fifth cause is the dreams that are not realised, the dreams that a person aspires and yearns for in this worldly life.

He has set up dreams for himself, dreams of the life that he would love to live. He imagines that it is within his capacity to realise these dreams for himself, but then the world surprises him with the opposite of what he was dreaming about. Several examples were given.

There are many people who fall into depression because of this collision that happens, between the dreams that they aspire to and the reality of the worldly life that surprises them.

This collision, very often, causes a kind of depression that takes hold of a person, and afflicts him with a dangerous illness.

There is no need to give more examples of the existentialists and existentialist philosophy, which is a consequence of this phenomenon and a result of this clash.

It would be more beneficial to move on to the treatment, which was introduced and briefly discussed in the last chapter. What is the treatment that a person can resort to in order to protect himself from depression when he is surprised by this cause?

The truth is that there are two treatments. The first treatment is what the psychologists call cognitive therapy, and it is that one should know the reality of this world and the universal laws that govern man,[42] and which man cannot control or hold sway over. In other words, it is embodied in man's knowing the identity of the world he lives in and the system upon which Allah ﷻ set it up. This will not happen unless the road to knowledge starts with the cognizance[43] of Allah, the belief that this world has a creator, and that the system that we see this world upon has someone who organises it and arranges it. This is the cognitive therapy.

When a person knows the reality of this world: its system, its laws, and its fixed principles, of which he will never be able to change a single thing, this cognitive therapy accomplishes a large part of the treatment.

It also accomplishes a large part of the protective means against this illness. In fact, it accomplishes the ridding of this illness, if it has afflicted a person and taken hold of him.

This cognitive therapy, however, depends on faith in Allah, sincere faith, not faith based on tradition and imitation. In other words, it depends on your knowing with absolute certainty that this universe is based on a system, and that the one who established it upon this system is Allah ﷻ.

42 i.e. Allah's *sunan*, which is how He deals with His slaves. The Imam has a book on this called *Min Sunan Illāhi fī ʿIbādihi*, an English translation of which is forthcoming.
43 Ar. *maʿrifah*.

Therefore, this worldly life is subject to this system that Allah ﷻ has established.You must know and understand this reality, via your faith in Allah, and via your certainty that Allah is Allah, that He is All-Wise, that He is Most Merciful, and know that this worldly life is just one chapter among the many chapters of a person's entire life story.

This worldly life is only the first chapter. It is followed by the second chapter, which is embodied by the life in the *barzakh*, the life that a person lives after death. That is followed by the third chapter, which is the Hereafter (*al-ḥayāt al-ākhirah*), where a person is settled and does not move on to any other life.

When you allow yourself to be sated by knowing this reality, you no longer hold your dreams in the same high regard, whether they have been realised or not. Who is going to fall victim to this clash, between the dreams that you aspire to and the reality of the world that has taken you by surprise? Who will be the victim of this clash?

You do not want to be the person who insists that this worldly life be according to his wishes and desires, and is not able to understand the cosmic reality that is compelling *him* to comply with the system of the world that Allah has established.

Yet, this is how it is for every individual who has veiled himself from Allah, and veiled himself from seeing Allah's laws in the universe, and imagines that "nature" is subject to "science". Therefore, it is within man's capacity to take hold of the reins of "science" and do whatever he wants with the world. This is what they imagine.

This delusion, however, does not survive. It is not long before a person finds a clash between his imagination and this worldly life. This worldly life that does not want to do what he wants, and does not want to be a ball that people toss back and forth. He therefore becomes the victim of depression.

The person who is veiled from Allah, and cannot see with his own insight – not his eyesight – that Allah's Hand is conducting this universe, and looks at this worldly life and imagines that because of his own knowledge and ability, and because civilisation has granted man this modern age; he thinks that he can squeeze out of this world whatever he wants. He thinks that he can subjugate it for whatever he wants. He thinks he can make it serve his dreams. This person will be taken by surprise by the complete opposite, and this is why he will become the victim of depression.

The parable of the person in this situation is a person who has been invited to a meal by a very generous man. He lays out a table for him that is replete with all kinds of food. These foods are new and strange; this person, who is a guest, knows nothing about them, and he does not know how to eat them. There are some foods that are only eaten cold. There are some foods that are only eaten warm. There are some foods whose peels are removed and only their cores are eaten, and there are other foods whose peels are eaten while their cores are disposed of.

Then there is a board that is set up next to this table. It is out of the host's perfect generosity that he has described and explained all of the foods on the table. He has named each one and explained how it is to be eaten; how that peel is eaten, how this core is eaten, how that food is eaten warm, this one is eaten cold, and so forth.

Imagine that some of the guests start eating right away. They do not look at this explanatory board at all. They sit at the table and start eating the food arbitrarily. Of course, when they see all this food, they think that they are going to eat delicious food, tasty food the likes of which they have never had, and they expect this luxury and comfort to last a long time.

However, when they start eating the various foods, without looking at how to eat them, they find that which they did not expect. They eat this food and it breaks their teeth. They eat that food cold when it should be eaten warm. They eat that which should be discarded, a peel that should be discarded, thinking that it is edible. Bitterness then fills their mouths and they feel nauseous, and so on.

They are shocked and surprised by this. Why? It is because they did not read the instructions on the board. In addition to becoming victims of their own ignorance, they try to justify their plight by saying that one of the most important things a person should know is that this table necessitates these pains, it necessitates these feelings, and necessitates patience with this bitterness.

This, according to them, is *predestination*, which is embodied in the necessity to be patient in the face of anxiety, ruin, despair, and so forth.

The truth, however, is that these people are the victims of their own ignorance. They should not have been the victims of ignorance since the cognitive therapy was there in front of them, but they ignored it.

The cognitive therapy could have been consumed within two minutes. All they had to do was stand in front of this board and learn about the different foods, and learn how they should be eaten. Then they could have enjoyed the foods without being made to choke. They could have achieved their gustatory dreams without any trouble or disturbance.

This worldly life is just like this. Allah ﷻ has sat us around the table of this worldly life. He has sent down to us a Book and an Elucidation. He has made clear therein how we are to deal with this worldly life, after explaining its nature. He has made it clear to us that this worldly life will not be as we desire. Rather, it is our desires that should be subordinate to what Allah ﷻ has established, and what He wills.

Thus, whoever studies these instructions before dealing with this worldly life, and knows how this chapter that we are living in is connected to the chapter that follows and the chapter that comes after that, matters will be easy for him, and the problems and calamities in front of him will be easy.

This person will not succumb to what is called depression, which secular societies are struggling with now to such an extent that there is a dramatic shortage of psychiatrists and other mental health professionals, and huge numbers of patients, every day, are crowding outside their clinics. [44]

The reason is that they do not know the reality of this worldly life. When people do not know the reality of this worldly life, they want to embrace it based on how it is in their dreams, not according to how it actually is.

This, therefore, is the first part of the cognitive therapy.

This cognitive therapy mitigates the problem; it does not put an end to it. If you know what this worldly life is, and how it is connected to what follows, and how to deal with it so that you protect yourself from that which is bad, like the example of the dinner table, you are then able to acquire a type of immunity against being afflicted with depression.

There is a supplement to this therapy. What is this supplement? The supplement, or second part, after having faith in Allah, true faith, which leads you to know the reality of this worldly life and its system, as well as Allah's ﷻ laws that govern it, is to do a lot of *dhikr* of Allah ﷻ.

44 Addressing the escalating psychiatrist shortage | AAMC https://www.aamc.org/news/addressing-escalating-psychiatrist-shortage, (Accessed 16 June, 2022).

You do a lot of *dhikr* of Allah ﷻ and you use your tongue to assist you in your *dhikr*. The *dhikr* on your tongue is good, but the *dhikr* on your tongue is only a means. A lot of *tasbīḥ* (saying *Subḥān Allah*), a lot of *istighfār* (saying *astaghfirullah*), a lot of *tawḥīd*, i.e. saying *la ilāha illa Allah*; all of these are some of the greatest means of drawing nearer to Allah. However, you need to know that this *dhikr* on the tongue is an anteroom leading to the *dhikr* of Allah in the heart, i.e. the heart's remembrance of Allah.

What does this *dhikr* do? It does what Allah says it does:

﴿ٱلَّذِينَ ءَامَنُوا وَتَطْمَئِنُّ قُلُوبُهُم بِذِكْرِ ٱللَّهِ ۗ
أَلَا بِذِكْرِ ٱللَّهِ تَطْمَئِنُّ ٱلْقُلُوبُ﴾

"Those who believe and whose hearts find peace in the remembrance of Allah. Know that only in the remembrance of Allah can the hearts find peace." [ar-Raᶜd 13:28]

These are Allah's words, which bear no discrepancy and no falsehood, in any way, shape, or form.

Know and be aware that in the remembrance of Allah, the hearts find peace.

Someone could say: 'What is the secret behind the *dhikr* of Allah and the heart finding peace? What is the connection? I remember Allah frequently. I remember Him here, I remember Him there, but what is the connection between my constant *dhikr* of Allah and the removal of pain and agony, and the feelings that push me into depression?'

Doing a lot of *dhikr* of Allah, with the heart, i.e. remembrance, gradually, will instil in you tremendous love for Allah ﷻ.

This can be summarised first and then explained in further detail. When the heart does a lot of *dhikr* of Allah, it causes the slave to love the Lord that he is remembering. If the love of Allah ﷻ is aroused within oneself, this love will overcome the whims and desires of the soul. This love will overcome any feelings of deprivation. This love will overcome the surprise and shock he feels when his dreams and ideas are contradicted by this worldly life.

The love of Allah overcomes. When the love of Allah overcomes, it expels these feelings of loss and deprivation, these feelings of grief, and the feelings caused by the clash between your dreams and the reality of this worldly life, which took you by surprise.

This is the summary.

What, however, is the evidence that your doing a lot of *dhikr* of Allah ﷻ will arouse the love of Allah within you?

The truth is that this is something self-evident. There is no need for analysis or elucidation.

Unfortunately, however, even though this matter is, in fact, self-evident, it does need to be elucidated for many people.

Think of it this way: if a person loves someone, it is for one of three reasons.

The first reason is beauty, which captivates the heart.

The second reason is *iḥsān* (beneficence), which takes over the soul's feelings, i.e. the soul tends to love the source that shows it kindness and generosity.

The third reason is sublimity (*ʿaẓamah*), which you see in various parts of the creation. This sublimity, whose appearance dazzles you and fills you with awe, makes your heart captive to this sublime thing, captive with love, along with veneration and esteem.

Therefore, there are three reasons why love is aroused within someone.

Think about a person who constantly remembers Allah ﷻ. Whenever his state changes, he is reminded of Allah. Whenever a blessing comes to him, he is reminded of Allah. Whenever he moves from one circumstance to another, when he is at home, when he is meeting people outside, in his relationships with others, he remembers Allah ﷻ. This situation awakens the three causes of love within this person. Your constant *dhikr* of Allah ﷻ wakes you up to the fact that Allah is the Uniquely Beautiful in existence.

If you remember Allah ﷻ frequently and then you enter a blooming garden, for example, which means that you look at the aromatic plants, you look at the roses and at the flowers, whose colours dazzle you with their beauty, you will immediately remember Allah ﷻ. You then move away from looking at these flowers and roses and aromatic plants, their colours and scents, and you abide with the One who coloured them. You abide with the One who scented them, who gave them these fragrances. You abide with the one who fashioned them and gave them this splendid and amazing appearance.

When you make a connection, via *dhikr*, between the image and the Maker of that image, it becomes impossible for you not to love Allah because of the first reason, which is that you have been nourished to love beauty. This is how everyone is.

When you look at the fruits that Allah has brought into creation, bearing all colours and various shapes and sizes, and all kinds of taste, and you remember Allah, you move from this sight to the

One who created this sight, from the image to the Maker of this image. You find yourself once again in front of the Beautiful, who unleashed the gifts of beauty where you are and throughout the entire world.

Furthermore, you find yourself in front of another motive, another motive that causes you to love Allah, and it is because of this first reason.

For example, have you ever opened a pomegranate? Have you split it into parts, and looked at its reddish-brown colour? Have you thought about when its seeds were planted, and where they were planted? Have you ever contemplated this beauty, which comes out of deep, dark soil? Have you ever contemplated this amazing structure?

When you look and contemplate, you move from the image to the Maker of this image. You always make that move. Then you roam and you find yourself swimming in an ocean overflowing with Allah's ﷻ beauty. How can you not love Him, the Uniquely Beautiful?

Your constant love of Allah ﷻ makes you love Allah for the first reason, which is beauty, because whatever beautiful image you see, you find that the image takes us to its Maker, that it takes us to its Originator, and that is Allah ﷻ.

If you are a merchant and you continue remembering Allah ﷻ and you see that your trade is profitable, you know that Allah is the One who has been beneficent towards you.

When you are ill and then you see that this illness has left you - you do not know how this illness managed to penetrate you, and you do not know how you extricated yourself from it - and you remember Allah – pay attention –, you constantly remember Allah, you know that a helping hand from Allah is what saved you from this.

When you look in the mirror, and you can see signs of health and well-being on your face and body, and you remember Allah ﷻ you remember the Uniquely Beneficent, i.e. Allah ﷻ.

When foods are placed in front of you when you are overcome with hunger, you look at these foods, and you think about how Allah has used His sky, how He has used His earth, and He has used His livestock, their meat and their udders, for your benefit, to satisfy your hunger.

When you look and you find that you enjoy this mouthful, and how Allah ﷻ separates from it that which will assist your well-being and removes that which is harmful or of no benefit; when you notice this happening day after day, and you remember Allah, you find yourself in front of another reason to love Allah, which is His beneficence. Allah is the Uniquely Beneficent. He is the Uniquely Beneficent.

Indeed, your remembrance of Allah will make you forget all these creations, these branches that serve you; you will look at them and only see the Uniquely Beneficent, who is Allah.

If a physician comes to you with his equipment and remedies and then you see that you have been cured, you will not look at the physician. Rather, you will look at the One who made the physician a physician. You will see Allah.

When you find someone who helps you and saves you from some affliction, and gets you out of it, you will not see this person but instead you will see Allah. Everything in existence is Allah's ﷻ soldiers.

And the list goes on. Therefore you must, inevitably, love Allah passionately. You began by loving Him for His beauty, and now you love Him for His beneficence.

If you constantly remember Allah ﷻ you will love Him for another reason, which is His sublimity.

Have you not looked at this universe? Have you not looked at its laws? Have you not looked at its dimensions and distances - which scientists describe in light years - the huge distances between meteors, the huge distances between galaxies, the huge distances between stars, and between those stars and galaxies and our earth?

Allah created all of this ﷻ. Therefore, the phenomena of this universe constitute a third factor that causes love for Allah ﷻ and is to love Him because He is Uniquely Sublime (*al-ʿAẓīm*).

Look at what *dhikr* does to your essence. Do not forget that the objective of remembrance is to be reminded, and that the tongue is an anteroom leading to the heart.

When you do abundant *dhikr* of Allah, the factors of love will be aroused, and there are three of them. The factors of love for Allah will be aroused within you. Therefore, if your heart is overflowing with love for Allah, this love will overcome any feelings of deprivation.

Suppose that this world does not realise your dreams. Suppose that this world makes you disfigured, for example – and we ask Allah for pardon and well-being, for all of us. Suppose that this world makes you poor. You were dreaming of getting married, of having a family, but this has not been realised, as many young people complain about.

What happens? Your intense love for Allah ﷻ - will not go so far as to make you forget. Rather, it will mitigate and continue to mitigate the pain of this deprivation. And you will feel that these feelings of deprivation are eclipsed by your love for Allah ﷻ and it will be as if you are saying to Allah ﷻ: 'My Lord, do what You want with me. I love you, and this love will console me and comfort me through any deprivation.'

Maybe you are a young person and you want to build the family of your dreams, to own the house that you dream of and imagine, and it is something you need. For whatever reason, however, this dream has not been realised. Your intense remembrance of Allah will make your heart a vessel for the love of Allah, and when you love Allah ﷻ your love for Allah is like an anaesthetic, like that which conceals the pain that a patient feels during a surgical operation.

Your intense love will make you forget huge amounts of this pain. It has been made clear to you that the remembrance of Allah is the source of the heart's finding peace and tranquillity. Go back to Allah's words:

﴿ٱلَّذِينَ ءَامَنُوا وَتَطْمَئِنُّ قُلُوبُهُم بِذِكْرِ ٱللَّهِ ۗ أَلَا بِذِكْرِ ٱللَّهِ تَطْمَئِنُّ ٱلْقُلُوبُ﴾

"Those who believe and whose hearts find peace in the remembrance of Allah. Know that only in the remembrance of Allah can the hearts find peace." [ar-Raʿd 13:28]

The heart finds peace because the one who remembers Allah comes to love Him ardently, and when he loves Allah ﷻ ardently he is willing to tolerate and even love whatever comes his way from his Lord, good or bad. Ardent lovers do this with the people they love, so why do we not expect them to do it with their Lord?

Praise be to Allah, Lord of all Creation.

Chapter Nine

The Fifth Cause:

The Inability To Achieve Personal Ambitions (Continued)

Cognitive-Behavioural Therapy: Part Two

The previous chapter talked about the fifth cause of depression and how there is both a cognitive therapy and a practical therapy. In summary, the cognitive therapy is embodied in man's knowing the truth about the world he lives in, which starts with the cognizance[45] of Allah and belief in Him, because He is the Creator of this world and He has established the system that this world follows.

After this cognizance of Allah, believing in Him, and knowing that this universe has a set system that we cannot override and is impossible to make yield to our dreams, comes behavioural therapy.

This second therapy is the abundant remembrance of Allah ﷻ. Remembrance of Allah means remembrance in the heart, although remembrance on the tongue is also a means to the heart's remembrance of Allah ﷻ. There is a connection between one's remembrance of Allah and the immunity one acquires against depression. We said that abundant remembrance of Allah stirs up the factors of

45 Ar. *maʿrifah*.

one's love for Allah ﷻ. If one loves Allah, that love will be one of the main factors that will mitigate the pain that results from the clash of one's dreams with the universal reality, which overpowers man.

At this point, some of us might say: 'You said, according to the Qurʾān, that the remembrance of Allah ﷻ brings peace to the heart:

﴿أَلَا بِذِكْرِ ٱللَّهِ تَطْمَئِنُّ ٱلْقُلُوبُ﴾

"Only in the remembrance of Allah can the heart find peace" [ar-Raʿd 13:28]

However, in another verse, Allah ﷻ says:

﴿إِنَّمَا ٱلْمُؤْمِنُونَ ٱلَّذِينَ إِذَا ذُكِرَ ٱللَّهُ وَجِلَتْ قُلُوبُهُمْ﴾

"The believers are those whose hearts tremble when Allah is mentioned" [al-Anfāl 8:2]

In this verse, Allah makes fear in the heart the result of remembering Him, and this fear, at least on the surface, contradicts the peace and tranquillity that we expect to find in the heart. Therefore, how can we accommodate both verses: "Only in the remembrance of Allah can the heart find peace" and "the believers are those whose hearts tremble when Allah is mentioned"?'

The answer is as follows. As for the first verse, the remembrance of Allah provides the heart with peace towards this worldly life with all its issues and its struggle with man. Those who increase their remembrance of Allah do not fall victim to depression because of poverty, a bodily calamity, or because one of their dreams did not come to fruition. The remembrance of Allah ﷻ steers a person away from the factors of stress, anxiety, and depression and provides him with peace and tranquillity regarding the worldly matters that he lives to achieve but are then not realised. In other words, due to your increased remembrance of Allah, a feeling of assurance that

Allah is merciful and wise is created within you. Regardless of the calamity, you think to yourself: 'This is what Allah has willed and there must be wisdom in it.'

Dhikr, as you now know, causes the factors of love for Allah to blossom within you. Therefore, whether life is good to you or not, whether you are in good health or not, or whether your relationships with people are good or you have enemies that envy you, none of this will immerse you in a state of depression or stress, and your heart will remain protected in peace.

As for the second verse, which says: "The believers are those whose hearts tremble when Allah is mentioned", according to the scholars, what is meant here by trembling heart is the intensity of feeling, emotion, and overall orientation towards what comes after death. 'Will Allah class me among those who are eternally happy or eternally wretched? If I am to be judged for my deeds tomorrow, will my good deeds outweigh my bad deeds or will it be the opposite? When people are crammed together as they cross the Sirat[46], will my feet stay firm? Will I pass that terrifying test?' Abundant *dhikr* of Allah ﷻ transports you from your concern about your worldly matters to being concerned about your Hereafter.

That was the meaning of the second verse and thus both verses are in perfect harmony. Remembrance of Allah gives us tranquillity in this life and in how we deal with it. Hence, let life be. That does not mean that you should wash your hands of this life completely, but rather, you should not worry about it. Remembrance of Allah also makes us anticipate what will happen after death. In other words, the remembrance of Allah keeps you busy with what you were created for, not with what Allah created for you.

---

46 Ar. *ṣirāṭ*. The *ṣirāṭ* is the bridge over the Fire that every human must pass on the Day of Resurrection; some make it while others do not. It is referred to in Sūrat Maryam 19:71 and is described in ḥadīths. See *Fatḥ al-ʿAlām bi Sharḥ Murshid al-ʿAnām* by Imam Muḥammad al-Jurdānī (Beirut: Dār Ibn Ḥazm, 1418/1997), 1:148-152.

For example, when you remember Allah frequently, this *dhikr* keeps you occupied with the duty that Allah has assigned you, and does not let you become preoccupied with what Allah has already guaranteed for you. The Creator ﷻ established you in this world and said to you: 'Look, I guarantee for you your livelihood, your provision, and your sufficiency if you adhere to this approach, but I demand some things from you'. Accordingly, your intellect tells you to stay busy with and focused on the duty that was given to you and not to worry about and preoccupy yourself with what Allah has guaranteed for you.

That was the meaning of Allah's statement in the first verse: "Only in the remembrance of Allah can the heart find peace"; the hearts are assured of what Allah has guaranteed for them. As for Allah's statement: "The believers are those whose hearts tremble when Allah is mentioned, whose faith is increased when His Signs are recited to them, and who put their trust in their Lord", what is meant here by "hearts tremble" is the concern about the duty that Allah has tasked you with.

Ibn ʿAṭāʾillāh al-Askandarī[47] ﵀ has some eloquent and wonderful words in this regard: "Your diligence in what is guaranteed for you and your falling short in what is required of you is evidence of your lack of insight." In other words, your diligence in worldly matters and your falling short in your duties to Allah is evidence of your lack of insight.

Most of us are guilty of this. We strive and exert a lot of effort into what Allah has guaranteed for us. Allah ﷻ says:

---

47 He is Tāj ad-Dīn Abū al-ʿAbbās Aḥmad ibn Muḥammad ibn ʿAbdul Karīm ibn ʿAṭāʾillāh al-Askandarī ash-Shādhilī, a master of various sciences, including *fiqh*, *uṣūl al-fiqh*, and *tafsīr*, and well-known *walī* of Allah, a scholar who acted upon his knowledge. His most famous works are his *Ḥikam*, which is a collection of wise statements, and *at-Tanwīr fī Isqāṭ at-Tadbīr*. He died in Cairo in the month of Jamāda al-Uwlā in the year 709AH (1309AD). See *Shajarat an-Nūr az-Zakiyyah fī Ṭabaqāt al-Mālikiyyah* by Shaykh Muḥammad Makhlūf (Beirut: Dār al-Kutub al-ʿIlmiyyah, 1424/2003), 1: 292-293.

﴿مَنْ عَمِلَ صَٰلِحًا مِّن ذَكَرٍ أَوْ أُنثَىٰ وَهُوَ مُؤْمِنٌ

فَلَنُحْيِيَنَّهُۥ حَيَوٰةً طَيِّبَةً﴾

"Anyone who acts rightly, male or female, being a believer, We will give them a good life." [An-Naḥl 16:97]

Allah has guaranteed this. However, we still strive for what Allah ﷻ has guaranteed for us, and we fall short or maybe even turn away from what Allah has required of us and commanded us to do.

What, then, is the remedy? The remedy is abundant remembrance of Allah. Your increased remembrance of Allah will make you feel assured of what Allah has guaranteed for you, and it will invigorate you, out of fear and dread, towards what Allah ﷻ has demanded from you. Therefore, these are detailed and accurate words without any uncertainty or contradiction in any way.

Therefore, the first therapy, which is the cognitive one, is understanding this universe as it really is, the way Allah has described it for us, and studying the laws and rules of this universe as He has revealed to us in His Book.

The second is behavioural therapy, which is to increase one's remembrance of Allah in the heart. In other words, by taking both these remedies or treatments, we connect all of our worldly circumstances and realities that we face, the blessings that surround us, and our daily practices with the Creator of all these realities and circumstances.

Someone might take both of these remedies and then say, 'I have tried this treatment but I am still in pain due to the calamity that has struck me. I am still in pain when I look at myself in the mirror and find that I am not as healthy-looking as my peers and friends.' A young man or woman might say something of this sort. 'I have used this treatment and I have increased my remembrance of

Allah. However, my basic desires continue to intensify because I am young, yet to be wed, and it looks like I will not be able to anytime soon, as long as my circumstances do not change and I continue to feel this pain. Therefore, the therapy that you have prescribed has not uprooted this illness.'

What is the answer to this question?

It should not be assumed that cognitive therapy, which is embodied in understanding the universe, and behavioural therapy, which is embodied in increasing one's remembrance of Allah, are a remedy for man to forget his misfortunes and for calamity to withdraw from his life. This is not what should be understood. Rather, it is a remedy for depression. Thus, whoever applies this treatment to himself will not fall victim to this illness called depression; this epidemic that is sweeping the secular, materialistic world, which in many cases causes its victims to resort to suicide.

When a person applies this treatment to himself, it protects him from this disease. As for completely removing calamity from people's lives, this would contradict Allah's universal law. If that were the case, what would necessitate the patience that Allah commanded of us?

This world is a place of affliction. One day is for you and one day is against you. Allah's system is summarised in His statement:

﴿وَنَبْلُوكُم بِٱلشَّرِّ وَٱلْخَيْرِ فِتْنَةً ۖ وَإِلَيْنَا تُرْجَعُونَ﴾

"We test you with both good and evil as a trial. And you will be returned to Us." [al-Anbiyā' 21:35]

Therefore, never expect or imagine that the entire world can be a type of paradise where you are always happy. This goes against the scheme and system that Allah has established this world upon. Why?

Man is a slave to Allah ﷻ, whether he acknowledges and admits it or not, and it is man's duty to implement his slavehood to Allah. As an adult, you must voluntarily, through your conduct, implement this slavehood, just as that slavehood was imposed upon you, involuntarily, when you were created to be a slave and it was embedded in your disposition. That is your task.

How does slavehood manifest in your life? The essence of slavehood and its qualities manifest inside of you through two things:

1. when you thank Allah for His blessings in times of ease,

2. when you turn to Allah and break down in front of Him in times of hardship.

When a person's life fully displays these two qualities, that is how he voluntarily declares his slavehood to Allah via his conduct. Please note these words. Thankfulness to Allah does not mean spoken words such as 'thanks be to Allah' or 'praise be to Allah'. Rather, what is meant by thankfulness is a person's conduct, which is manifested in his patience and his gratitude to Allah ﷻ.

For example, Allah has blessed you with the sense of eyesight. Therefore, your gratitude to Him for this blessing is to use your eyes for what Allah has asked of you. Allah has blessed you with wealth, and therefore your gratitude for the blessing of wealth is to use it and manage it in the manner Allah has asked of you.

These applications represent the first half of the behavioural and voluntary slavehood to Allah ﷻ. Patience during calamities, turning to Allah, beautiful forbearance[48], and contentment with Him represent the second half.

48 Ar. *ṣabr jamīl*; see Sūrat Yūsuf 12:18.

How can you be both patient and grateful simultaneously? This can only be when your life and the world you live in are full of blessings that necessitate gratitude and calamities that require patience. Calamities and hardships are thus inevitable. However, man is faced with two scenarios:

1. Either you are overwhelmed by these calamities, which cause you dangerous ailments that can propel you to madness or even incite you to suicide, or

2. These misfortunes are continually reduced and mitigated in your eyes and you view them as a patient would view his bitter medicine. You taste its bitterness, but at the same time, you are happy that you are being healed and this treatment does not annihilate you in any way.

Therefore, a person can be in either one of those two scenarios.

When can you deal with your misfortunes the same way a patient would deal with his bitter medicine? This is only possible when you are cognizant of Allah, when you trust in Him, and do a lot of *dhikr*. You will thus love Allah and trust in Him. At that point, you are freed from the illness of depression but you are not freed from the pain of the calamity. The calamity remains but its effect weakens, and it becomes exactly as described above; like bitter medicine to a patient or perhaps something more serious, like surgery to a patient who has surrendered to his surgeon.

Now, comes the role of the other remedy for calamities, which is the remedy of patience. What is meant by patience? Patience is when man controls himself and stands firm and perseveres in the face of what he dislikes, hoping for some bliss and delight that will follow. That is patience.

However, there is no point in being patient with a calamity when there is no benefit to be had. For example, only a humiliated person puts up with oppression or injustice. It is important to understand the difference.

Therefore, when you face a hardship that distresses you, you know that Allah has made you a firm promise to grant you reward, merit, and happiness if you show beautiful patience. Thus, you say: 'All right, I will be patient.' However, your patience will be similar to that of a fasting person who is patient with thirst and hunger because he knows that in a few hours he will break his fast. That is the meaning of patience. Similarly, a believer experiences a calamity and undoubtedly feels its impact, but its impact keeps easing and diminishing and becomes just like bitter medicine or even surgery for a patient.

The Ambition to Get Married

Now, let us look at the concerns of some young people, specifically regarding their inability to get married which was touched upon earlier in the chapter. A young man might say, 'I never want to disobey Allah. I am not tempted by the love of a girl or anything like that. However, I suffer from what every man suffers from. I feel the need for a tranquil dwelling, as Allah has said. I feel the need for marriage and a family because I am human. However, when I look around me, I find that all the avenues to that are closed off to me.'

He might then add and say, 'This urgent need along with my adherence to Allah's commands creates another cause, and a very serious one, that makes me depressed. It makes me feel that I am estranged from society. Everyone around me is happy. They are fortunate and prosperous. They enjoy their natural inclinations. As for myself, I am far removed from them; I do not have any of these things. I live on the periphery of life. I mull over my dreams. This situation makes me feel like I am living in exile. This exile, slowly but surely, is forcing me into a state of depression. At the same time, you claim that there are remedies and treatments that prevent depression.'

There are many people who illustrate this state in various ways, and there is no doubt about their truthfulness in what they are saying.

However, it is as if he is confusing the disease of depression with the occurrence of calamity. This young man will never fall into depression if he truly believes in Allah. He will not fall into depression if he is certain that Allah is wise. However, he will suffer and he will feel pain, perhaps even agonising pain.

So, what can be said to these young people?

This problem is indeed a serious problem. A human being is a human being. He is like anyone else; he needs to satisfy his natural inclinations, and it is a serious problem if he is not able to. However, it must be emphasised to you that this major problem is made much smaller and wanes when a person resorts to the treatment that was discussed in the previous chapters.

If you are in this situation, the question is: have you sought refuge in Allah, in the morning and in the evening? Have you presented these complaints at His door? Have you done so persistently, without interruption, and this problem is still weighing you down?

It is obvious that you have not done this. There is no doubt that those who seek refuge in Allah ﷻ and flee from these dreams of theirs to Allah's magnanimity, and to His doorstep, with perseverance and persistence, who complain to Him and implore Him, and supplicate to Him; there is no doubt that those who do this find the weight of this affliction to be mitigated, that its impact is lessened. No one is saying that it goes away. It does not go away.

However, Allah ﷻ makes this person feel more relaxed, more reassured, and this helps him withstand and resist this situation, such that this person does not fall into depression.

It will not be possible for you to mull over your pain, nor mull over your afflictions in any way, shape, or form, such that it leads to depression unless you allow yourself to fall into one situation and one situation alone, which is that you forget Allah ﷻ and you do not sincerely turn to Allah ﷻ.

These young people should be told what Allah has said,

﴿وَلَنَبْلُوَنَّكُم بِشَىْءٍ مِّنَ ٱلْخَوْفِ وَٱلْجُوعِ وَنَقْصٍ مِّنَ ٱلْأَمْوَٰلِ وَٱلْأَنفُسِ وَٱلثَّمَرَٰتِ ۗ وَبَشِّرِ ٱلصَّٰبِرِينَ﴾

"We will test you with a certain amount of fear and hunger and loss of wealth and life and fruits. But give good news to the steadfast." [al-Baqarah 2:155]

Allah commanded His Messenger ﷺ to give glad tidings specifically to those who are steadfast and patient. Allah also said that He will honour His steadfast and patient slaves with reward on the Day of Resurrection without being held accountable, meaning He will never call them to account.

﴿إِنَّمَا يُوَفَّى ٱلصَّٰبِرُونَ أَجْرَهُم بِغَيْرِ حِسَابٍ﴾

"The steadfast will be paid their wages in full without any reckoning." [az-Zumar 39:10]

Therefore, all of us will experience calamity and we are all susceptible to calamities. Calamities, however, are a spectrum. Some of them are of vivid colours while some are invisible. Allah ﷻ allocates blessings to people just as He allocates calamities and hardships. However, what reduces the impact of calamity? As was stated before, the increase in remembrance of Allah to the extent that this remembrance stimulates the love of Allah within you. If you love Allah, your love for Him will defeat what this calamity has made you feel.

The other thing that will mitigate the impact of calamity is turning to Allah in supplication. Supplicate to Allah ﷻ, turn to Him, and implore Him. Read Allah's statement:

﴿أَمَّن يُجِيبُ ٱلْمُضْطَرَّ إِذَا دَعَاهُ وَيَكْشِفُ ٱلسُّوٓءَ وَيَجْعَلُكُمْ خُلَفَآءَ ٱلْأَرْضِ ۗ أَءِلَٰهٌ مَّعَ ٱللَّهِ﴾

"He Who responds to the oppressed when they call on Him and removes their distress, and has appointed you as vicegerents[49] on the earth. Is there another god besides Allah?" [an-Naml 27:62]

This verse is in the form of a question, and the question indicates that the context of the verse is self-evident. It is as if Allah ﷻ is saying that His response to the supplication of the needy is a foregone conclusion. Therefore, who is it that answers the oppressed and desperate? It is Allah ﷻ.

Thus, when you are desperate, do you turn to Allah in the middle of the night or pre-dawn hours, the times when Allah calls on His slaves?

It has been narrated that the Messenger of Allah ﷺ said: {Allah provides respite until a half or two thirds of the night have passed. Then He says: "My slave does not ask of anyone other than Me. Whoever calls upon Me, I will answer him; whoever asks of Me, I will give him; whoever asks My forgiveness, I will forgive him," until dawn comes.}[50]

49 Ar. *khulafā'*.
50 *Sunan Ibn Mājah*, Ḥadīth no. 1367.

Do you wake up at this blessed time, while those that are astray and unaware of Allah are asleep, and the places of sin (pubs, bars, clubs etc.) have closed for the night? Do you speak to Allah ﷻ and plead with Him? If you make pleading with Allah a regular *wird*,[51] Allah will relieve you of your unease and grant you a way out of your distress. You must be certain of this.

In summary, calamity, along with its effect on man, has been distinguished from depression. Calamity is a common denominator for all humanity, from the Messengers and Prophets through to the masses. However, calamities are diverse, and can be hidden or invisible on many occasions. As for depression, it afflicts man and turns into an illness that has dangerous and horrific consequences for him. The remedy for this disease is in the Book of Allah ﷻ. Those who take what is in the Qurʾān upon themselves and commit to the Qurʾānic remedies that have been mentioned, Allah protects them against the illness of depression.

This is one thing. The second thing, which constitutes a conclusion to the treatment, is that the community is responsible. There are individual problems that the individual and the community work together towards solving. The individual's duty is to turn to Allah, to submit to Him and be patient, and to adhere to Allah's words ﷻ:

﴿وَلْيَسْتَعْفِفِ ٱلَّذِينَ لَا يَجِدُونَ نِكَاحًا حَتَّىٰ يُغْنِيَهُمُ ٱللَّهُ مِن فَضْلِهِۦ﴾

"Those who cannot find the means to marry should be abstinent until Allah enriches them from His bounty."
[an-Nūr 24:33]

As for the role of the community, it is to have mercy on these people, to be compassionate with them. The community must not withdraw from this obligation, and neglect to carry out this

51 Ar. *wird*, which can be daily portions of the Qurʾān, supplications (*duʿāʾ*), and remembrances (*adhkār*). Please see the book *Remembrances & Etiquettes of the Prophet* ﷺ.

responsibility. What is the community? It is the individual multiplied. The community is the crowds of people whose groups and individuals work together according to a certain communal approach. This is a community.

Allah always establishes the community. This is Allah's standard practice (*sunnah*) in the universe. It is established in different types and forms. It varies, and sometimes certain parts do not agree with other parts. In a community, there are wealthy people who live in luxury. Then there are those who have less, those whose wealth is average. And then there are those who are poor. This is because Allah's standard practice is in effect, in accordance with His words:

﴿وَجَعَلْنَا بَعْضَكُمْ لِبَعْضٍ فِتْنَةً أَتَصْبِرُونَ ۗ وَكَانَ رَبُّكَ بَصِيرًا﴾

"But We have made some of you a trial for others to see if you will be steadfast. Your Lord sees everything."
[al-Furqān 25:20]

Furthermore, the community is subject to Allah's words ﷻ:

﴿...وَرَفَعْنَا بَعْضَهُمْ فَوْقَ بَعْضٍ دَرَجَٰتٍ لِّيَتَّخِذَ بَعْضُهُم بَعْضًا سُخْرِيًّا ۗ وَرَحْمَتُ رَبِّكَ خَيْرٌ مِّمَّا يَجْمَعُونَ﴾

"...and He raised some of them above others in rank so that some of them are subservient to others. But the mercy of your Lord is better than anything they amass."
[az-Zukhruf 43:32]

Thus, it is inevitable that you will find people at different levels, in terms of their power and in terms of their wealth. This is so that the rich can be tested by the poor and the poor can be tested by the rich.

Then Allah ﷻ has established a Revealed Law for them, and He has commanded them to conduct themselves according to a certain approach. He has given them a scale of justice and He has commanded them to judge all of their behaviour according to this scale.

Then Allah has commanded them to show mercy to one another, and He has told them, on the tongue of His Messenger, Muḥammad ﷺ:

{Whoever does not show mercy is not shown mercy.}[52]

When the community carries out its responsibility,[53] and the individual, also, carries out the aforementioned objective, the problem disappears.

However, if the community is falling short, the other part of the treatment remains and you, as an individual, are responsible for it. You ask Allah, you supplicate to Him, you seek refuge in Him, and from that you make a regular, daily *wird*, which is never interrupted. The weight of this affliction will then be mitigated for you. You will mull over it, but it will not turn into depression.

Someone might ask: "Should your claim prevent us from seeing mental health professionals?[54] If we are aware and we believe that the Qurʾān contains the cure, does this belief prevent us from seeing mental health professionals?" In principle, no. It should not.[55]

The Messenger ﷺ said: {Allah has sent down both the disease and the cure, and He has appointed a cure for every disease, so treat yourselves medically...}[56]

---

52 Related by al-Bukhārī (Ḥadīth no. 5997) and Muslim (Ḥadīth no. 2318), as well as others.
53 The responsibility of the community is to facilitate marriage, and it starts with parents.
54 e.g. psychologists.
55 Some people suffer from some severe types of depression, such as Major Depressive Disorder, and would be best advised to consult a mental health professional.
56 *Sunan Abī Dāwūd*, Ḥadīth no. 3874.

However, what is true for bodily diseases is not exactly true for mental illnesses. There is a huge difference between bodily diseases, which doctors find cures for easily because they can quickly discover what they are after a check up and provide a diagnosis. This is because they are subject to the body and matter. Furthermore, there are plenty of medical devices that detect the intricacies of matter.

However, this does not apply to mental illness. Until now, "science" has not been able to find devices that monitor and detect the "*nafs*"; i.e. the soul.[57]

57 See Appendix D: Mental Illness.

Chapter Ten
Is Sorcery[58]
A Cause of Depression?

After discussing the topic of depression at length, there remains two fundamental questions, one being the branch of the other, that need to be answered.

The branch question is: 'Isn't sorcery (*siḥr*), also, one of the causes of depression?' In other words, is not sorcery one of the causes that necessitates a person's exposure to depression?

Of course, among the five causes of depression that have been enumerated, sorcery is not one of them.

So, what is the answer to this question?

To answer the branch question, we have to answer the root question:

Does sorcery exist?

Yes, it does indeed exist. How can it not exist when the Qurʾān has spoken about it, and in more than one place? However, what does it mean that sorcery exists? Does it mean that sorcery is

58 Ar. *siḥr*.

something that has the capacity to invert reality? Does it mean that it is possible for sorcery to make something existent not exist, or something non-existent exist?

No. This is not what is meant when it is said that sorcery exists. Rather, what is meant is that the scope of sorcery's existence is confined to making people imagine that something is there when it actually is not. It makes a person's mind and intellect think that things that have no reality are actually present.

This is one thing. The other thing is that sorcery could hold sway over a person's body and afflict it with some sort of harm or illness. Therefore, sorcery is like germs or microbes, or the material causes that cause various illnesses in the body.

This is the scope within which the existence of sorcery can be explained. As for what is beyond that, sorcery does not have a reality. That is, sorcery does not possess the ability to invert reality. It cannot bring something non-existent into existence, or take something existent out of existence.

This point can be emphasised by paying attention and listening to Allah's ﷻ words. Allah ﷻ says about Firʿawn's sorcerers:

﴿...فَلَمَّآ أَلْقَوْا۟ سَحَرُوٓا۟ أَعْيُنَ ٱلنَّاسِ وَٱسْتَرْهَبُوهُمْ وَجَآءُو بِسِحْرٍ عَظِيمٍ﴾

"...they cast a spell on the people's eyes and caused them to feel great fear of them. They produced an extremely powerful magic." [al-ʾAʿrāf 7:116]

'They' refers to Firʿawn's sorcerers; they cast a spell on the people's eyes. Pay attention to this expression. The sorcery did not make the ropes transform into snakes. Rather, the sorcery made their eyes imagine that the ropes had turned into snakes, but they never did.

This understanding is found elsewhere in the Qurʾān, in Sūrat Ṭaha, when Allah says:

﴿قَالُوا يَٰمُوسَىٰٓ إِمَّآ أَن تُلْقِيَ وَإِمَّآ أَن نَّكُونَ أَوَّلَ مَنْ أَلْقَىٰ ﴿٦٥﴾ قَالَ بَلْ
أَلْقُواۖ فَإِذَا حِبَالُهُمْ وَعِصِيُّهُمْ يُخَيَّلُ إِلَيْهِ مِن سِحْرِهِمْ أَنَّهَا تَسْعَىٰ﴾

"They said: 'Mūsā, will you throw or shall we be the first to throw?' He said: 'No, you throw!' And suddenly their ropes and staff appeared to him [*yukhayyalu ilayhi*], by their sorcery, to be slithering about." [Ṭaha 20:65-66]

They *appeared* to him, because of their sorcery, to be slithering about.

Sorcery, therefore, exists but only to this extent. That is, it is a phenomenon that controls a person's mind such that he imagines things to be other than what they truly are.

And maybe sorcery will affect a person's body, just as natural phenomena affect it, like germs, microbes, and so forth, and therefore the person experiences some type of pain or illness.

Furthermore, this sorcery, whatever its scope may be, cannot produce any effect without Allah's permission. It cannot produce any effect whatsoever. It is just like all other material means. Water cannot quench thirst without Allah's permission. Food cannot satiate without Allah's permission. Microbes cannot attack your body without Allah's ﷻ permission. The same goes for sorcery.

Allah ﷻ says about sorcery, as well as its origin, in a long verse:

﴿وَٱتَّبَعُوا مَا تَتْلُوا ٱلشَّيَٰطِينُ عَلَىٰ مُلْكِ سُلَيْمَٰنَۖ وَمَا كَفَرَ سُلَيْمَٰنُ
وَلَٰكِنَّ ٱلشَّيَٰطِينَ كَفَرُوا يُعَلِّمُونَ ٱلنَّاسَ ٱلسِّحْرَ وَمَآ أُنزِلَ عَلَى

ٱلْمَلَكَيْنِ بِبَابِلَ هَـٰرُوتَ وَمَـٰرُوتَ ۚ وَمَا يُعَلِّمَانِ مِنْ أَحَدٍ حَتَّىٰ يَقُولَآ
إِنَّمَا نَحْنُ فِتْنَةٌ فَلَا تَكْفُرْ ۖ فَيَتَعَلَّمُونَ مِنْهُمَا مَا يُفَرِّقُونَ بِهِۦ
بَيْنَ ٱلْمَرْءِ وَزَوْجِهِۦ ۚ وَمَا هُم بِضَآرِّينَ بِهِۦ مِنْ أَحَدٍ إِلَّا بِإِذْنِ ٱللَّهِ ۚ
وَيَتَعَلَّمُونَ مَا يَضُرُّهُمْ وَلَا يَنفَعُهُمْ ۚ وَلَقَدْ عَلِمُوا۟ لَمَنِ ٱشْتَرَىٰهُ مَا لَهُۥ فِى
ٱلْـَٔاخِرَةِ مِنْ خَلَـٰقٍ ۚ وَلَبِئْسَ مَا شَرَوْا۟ بِهِۦٓ أَنفُسَهُمْ ۚ لَوْ كَانُوا۟ يَعْلَمُونَ ﴾

"They follow what the shayṭāns recited in the reign of Sulaymān. Sulaymān did not disbelieve but the shayṭāns did, teaching people sorcery and what had been sent down to Hārūt and Mārūt, the two angels in Babylon, who taught no one without first saying to him: 'We are merely a trial and temptation, so do not disbelieve.' People learned from them how to separate between a man and his wife, but they cannot harm anyone by it except with Allah's permission. They have learned what will harm them and will not benefit them. They know that any who deal in it will have no share in the Hereafter. What an evil thing they have sold themselves for if they only knew." [al-Baqarah 2:102]

Two things have been established: sorcery exists but within a limited scope. It makes the mind believe that something is such. It gives a person the impression that something is other than what it truly is. It can also have an effect on a person's body, just as various material things that can have an effect on the body.

The second thing is that this sorcery cannot produce any effect in a person, or create separation between a man and his wife, or make him experience any sort of depression, unless it is by Allah's ﷻ permission and by His planning and creation.

If we know this, we can answer the question that has been asked: is not sorcery also one of the causes of depression?

The answer is as follows:

Sorcery cannot affect a person unless Allah commands it, unless Allah ﷻ allows it. It cannot be emphasised enough that anyone who adheres to Allah's ﷻ commands, follows Allah's ﷻ path, and enjoins upon himself a portion of the Qur'ān that he recites every day, as well as regular *awrād*[59] that have been passed down from the Messenger of Allah ﷺ along with regular *dhikr* of Allah ﷻ; it is not possible for sorcery to affect this person *at all.*

This is a fact that you must know and understand. Close your eyes and imagine. Is there someone who has been afflicted by sorcery, in whatever way, and he is someone who adheres to Allah's commands? Is he someone who regularly recites Allah's Book? Is he someone who has a regular *wird*, consisting of *dhikr* and supplications that have been passed down from the Messenger of Allah ﷺ, that he ﷺ would regularly say, every morning and evening? A person like this will never be afflicted by sorcery.

Rather, sorcery can have an effect on those who stray from Allah's ﷻ path. This is exactly how the Messenger of Allah ﷺ described it:

{The wolf eats the sheep that is far removed.}[60] That is, it eats the one that is straying.

Is there any evidence for this?

Indeed, there is. Look at Allah's ﷻ words:

---

59 This is the plural of *wird*.

60 This is Ḥadīth no. 1086 in the Dār al-Minhāj edition of *Riyāḍ as-Ṣāliḥīn*, 372. One can also see *Sunan Abī Dāwūd*, Ḥadīth no. 547.

﴿وَإِمَّا يَنزَغَنَّكَ مِنَ ٱلشَّيْطَٰنِ نَزْغٌ فَٱسْتَعِذْ بِٱللَّهِ ۚ إِنَّهُۥ سَمِيعٌ عَلِيمٌ ﴿٢٠٠﴾ إِنَّ
ٱلَّذِينَ ٱتَّقَوْا۟ إِذَا مَسَّهُمْ طَٰٓئِفٌ مِّنَ ٱلشَّيْطَٰنِ تَذَكَّرُوا۟ فَإِذَا هُم مُّبْصِرُونَ﴾

"If an evil impulse from Shayṭān provokes you, seek refuge in Allah. He is All-Hearing, All-Knowing." As for those who have taqwā, when they are bothered by visitors from Shayṭān, they remember – i.e. they remember Allah – and immediately see clearly." [al-ʾAʿrāf 7:200-201]

He ﷻ also says:

﴿فَإِذَا قَرَأْتَ ٱلْقُرْءَانَ فَٱسْتَعِذْ بِٱللَّهِ مِنَ ٱلشَّيْطَٰنِ ٱلرَّجِيمِ ﴿٩٨﴾ إِنَّهُۥ
لَيْسَ لَهُۥ سُلْطَٰنٌ عَلَى ٱلَّذِينَ ءَامَنُوا۟ وَعَلَىٰ رَبِّهِمْ يَتَوَكَّلُونَ ﴿٩٩﴾ إِنَّمَا
سُلْطَٰنُهُۥ عَلَى ٱلَّذِينَ يَتَوَلَّوْنَهُۥ وَٱلَّذِينَ هُم بِهِۦ مُشْرِكُونَ﴾

"Whenever you recite the Qurʾān, seek refuge in Allah from the accursed Shayṭān. He has no authority – i.e. Shayṭān has no authority – **over those who believe and put their trust in their Lord. He only has authority over those who take him as a friend and associate others with Allah."**
[an-Naḥl 16:98-100]

This is what Allah ﷻ says. These are Allah's words; they must not be doubted. If we believe that these are Allah's words, can there be any discrepancy in them? Contemplate this clear speech:

"Whenever you recite the Qurʾān, seek refuge in Allah from the accursed Shayṭān. He has no authority over those who believe and put their trust in their Lord. He only has authority over those who take him as a friend – i.e. they follow him – and associate others with Allah."
[an-Naḥl 16:98-100]

To those who ask if sorcery is a cause of depression: do not go outside of Allah's shelter and protection. Fortify yourselves, as much as you are able to, with the fortress of adhering to Allah's commands and staying away from what He has prohibited. Moreover, be consistent with your daily *awrād*, such as reciting Allah's ﷻ Book and repeating the supplications and remembrances that have been transmitted to us from the Messenger of Allah ﷺ, which he ﷺ consistently recited in the morning and evening. You will find that sorcery will not be able to be a cause of depression, no matter how much sorcerers and charlatans may try. You will remain far removed from their effects, fortified against their plots.

This is one thing. The other thing is that when it is said that sorcery exists, the sorcery that exists in proportion to the pure deceit and trickery that has become worse in our Arabic and Islamic societies represents one in a thousand. As for what is beyond this one in a thousand, all of it is deceit and lies, and words that have no reality whatsoever. There are those who make people believe things, who dupe and deceive. There are those who make this subject a means to earn money, to make a living, and they often work together. They will make people believe that a certain individual has been afflicted with sorcery. Then their accomplices will offer a cure and make people believe that he has been cured, after charging a good price, of course. Then they divide the money amongst themselves. Do not waste your time worrying about this.

Nevertheless, if you think that you may have been harmed by something like this, the advice is as follows: if you have indeed been harmed, know that you are straying from Allah's path. Know that you are not adhering to Allah's ﷻ commands. Return to Allah's path. Seek refuge in Allah. Carry out His commands. Enjoin upon yourself some type of *wird*, as much as you are able, that consists of reciting the Qurʾān, remembering Allah, and repeating what the Messenger of Allah ﷺ would repeat, such as:

أَعُوذُ بِكَلِمَاتِ اللهِ التَّامَّاتِ مِنْ شَرِّ مَا خَلَقَ

{I seek refuge in Allah's complete Words from the evil that He has created.}[61]

This is part of what the Messenger of Allah ﷺ would repeat. You will find that you are fortified against that which you are afraid of.

There remains, however, one more thing that has to be said.

You should not resort to this treatment the same way a patient resorts to a doctor that he has no personal relationship with. He knocks on his door for a sole purpose; to get a cure for himself. He takes the medicine and then, if he gets better, he stops taking it and moves on with his life, because his relationship with the doctor has come to an end.

If you want to use the treatment in Allah's Book, and to seek refuge in these *awrād* and remembrances, in this way, know that Allah ﷻ is never deceived, at all. The motive for seeking refuge in Allah should be the motive of slavehood to Allah ﷻ. In other words, you should know that in every situation and circumstance, if you are exposed to sorcery or not, if you are exposed to illnesses or not, if you are exposed to tyrants and oppressors or not; in all your vicissitudes and states, you are never independent of Allah's care. You are never independent of Allah's protection over you, even when you are in your bed, when you are in your own house, when you are in the room that you sleep in. You are not independent of Allah's ﷻ protection over you. If Allah ﷻ were to abandon you, there are endless ways that can potentially lead to your destruction.

This air that we breathe and surrounds us is full of bacteria and germs. It is full of microbes, in every single moment. When you breathe, the process of inhaling and exhaling exposes you to all

61 Related by Muslim, Ḥadīth no. 2708; at-Tirmidhī, Ḥadīth no. 3437; Ibn Mājah, Ḥadīth no. 3547, and others.

kinds of illnesses. However, Allah always protects you from them with what they call the immune system. Ask any doctor: what is the immune system? What does it mean? You will not find any meaning for this expression, other than it is Allah's ﷻ protection.

There is no situation in which a person does not need Allah and then another situation in which he does need Allah عَزَّ وَجَلَّ. In every moment, you are in Allah's grip. If Allah were to abandon you for one moment, you would just be swept away by the wind. Have you not read Allah's عَزَّ وَجَلَّ words when He talks about the blessings He bestows upon man?

﴿لَهُۥ مُعَقِّبَٰتٌ مِّنۢ بَيْنِ يَدَيْهِ وَمِنْ خَلْفِهِۦ يَحْفَظُونَهُۥ مِنْ أَمْرِ ٱللَّهِ﴾

"Everyone has a succession of protectors in front of him and behind him, guarding him by Allah's command."
[ar-Raᶜd 13:11]

That is, every person has protection, guarding him, and it consists of angels and of that which we do not know, in front of him and behind him.

This protection is because of a command from Allah ﷻ.

It is a superficial fool who imagines that he does not need to seek refuge in Allah when he cannot see any enemies around him, he cannot find any sorcerers plotting against him, and he cannot find any illness infiltrating his body. He has his wealth. He has his health. He is in a fortress of comfort and well-being, and therefore he does not need to seek refuge in Allah.

These are the thoughts of a foolish man. In any moment, anything can happen to you. As mentioned above, this air that surrounds you; if Allah did not protect you from what it contains, you would be destroyed. Ask scientists and scholars about this and they will tell you.

This is the answer to the question. The truth is that sorcery is not one of the causes of depression, because most of what is called sorcery is actual trickery and deceit.

If there is any hidden, true sorcery, the way to save yourself is to seek refuge in Allah, to adhere to Allah's commands, and not to stray from Allah's door. Then, make a daily *wird* for yourself, which you repeat every day, consisting of reciting Allah's ﷻ Book and the remembrances and supplications that have been transmitted to us from the Messenger of Allah ﷺ, which he ﷺ would adhere to.

And with Allah alone is every success.

Appendix A

Causes of Depression and Their Remedies

1. Not Knowing the Reality of Life	
Remedy 1	Know that this universe has a Creator, that it has a Sustainer who originated and organised it.
	Understand that Allah has programmed His universe according to a system, and that He has established and assigned you with a task.
Remedy 2	Listen and pay attention to Allah's speech regarding man's creation, the story behind man's existence, man's task and obligations, and his conclusion.
	Know the story of your existence in this universe, and know how existence started and where it will end.
	Know that death is not an end, and that you shall return to Allah.

2. Fear of the Future & Failure	
Remedy	Follow Allah's command to work and not to resort to idleness or unemployment.
	Then, trust in Allah and leave the result of your work to Him. He is the guarantor of your happiness.
	Know that your work is not what maintains your livelihood, your business is not what makes you happy, and your work on the land, growing crops and raising animals, is not what enriches you and provides for you, rather it is Allah.
3. Fear of Adversity and Affliction	
Remedy 1	To know that all afflictions, before they came, were decreed and ordained.
	Do not say: 'If only I had done such-and-such, this affliction would not have happened'.
	If it does not happen because of this reason, Allah will create another reason.
Remedy 2	Know the insignificance of this life, and that this is not the life that you should embrace.
	This life is just a passage to a destination.

Remedy 3	If life makes you weep one day, it will make you laugh tomorrow.
	Do not expect to be happy all the time. Do not expect everything to be beautiful all the time.
	Remember Allah's reward for those who are patient in bad times and thankful in good times.
3.1. Having no Hope of Forgiveness	
Remedy	Know that Allah forgives all sins.
	Know that one of the greatest proofs of Allah's love for you is that you turned to Him with repentance and you returned to Him.
	If Allah did not love you, He would not have placed disgust for these sins in your heart and the yearning to repent to Him.
	Strengthen your faith and repentance to Allah with knowledge, by approaching and contemplating Allah's Book, understanding its meanings as well as approaching the ḥadīths of the Messenger of Allah ﷺ.

4. Fear of Death	
Remedy	Understand that death does not mean non-existence.
	Know that man remains binary in his constitution, composed of both a body and a spirit. The spirit lives on and its connection with the body remains after death.
	Death is a person's drawing nearer to Allah, a person's moving to Allah's magnanimity and reward.
	Place between yourself and death a path that is paved with sincere slavehood to Allah, a path that is paved with repentance to Allah.
	Death is a key to Paradise, a key to bliss, a key to achieving nearness to Allah.
5. The Inability To Achieve Personal Ambitions	
Remedy	Have sincere belief in Allah ﷻ, the Creator of this universe and trust in His wisdom and mercy.
	Practice *dhikr*, i.e. remembrance of Allah ﷻ.
	Remember Allah always in all situations that you come across in life.

Cognitive Therapy	Know with absolute certainty that this universe is based on a system, and that the one who established it upon this system is Allah, Glorified and Exalted is He.
	Know what this worldly life is, and how it is connected to what follows. Do not embrace it based on how it is in your dreams.
	Have faith in Allah, true faith, which leads to knowing the reality of this worldly life and its system, as well as Allah's laws, Glorified and Exalted is He, that govern it.
Behavioural Therapy	Do a lot of *dhikr* of Allah. Remembrance will gradually instil in you tremendous love for Allah.
	The love of Allah overcomes and expels the feelings of loss, deprivation, grief, and the feelings caused by the clash between your dreams and the reality of this worldly life.
	Abundant *dhikr* of Allah ﷻ transports you from your concern about your worldly matters to being concerned about your Hereafter.
	Your increased remembrance of Allah will make you feel assured of what Allah has guaranteed for you, and it will invigorate you, out of fear and dread, towards what Allah ﷻ has demanded from you.
	Link everything in your life, the blessings that surround you, and everything you do with the Creator of this life and its circumstances.

	Thank Allah for His blessings in times of ease.
	Turn to Allah and break down in front of Him in times of hardship.
	Be patient during calamities, turn to Allah, and have beautiful forbearance and contentment with Him.
	Turn to Allah in supplication in the middle of the night or pre-dawn hours.

Appendix B
Man's Love for Allah
By Imam Muḥammad Saʿīd Ramaḍān al-Būṭī[62]

Just as we have seen verses in the Qur'ān that affirm Allah's love for man in both of its types: the pre-eternal, inherent love and the earned, contingent love, we can also see verses that affirm man's love for Allah and in both of its types: the ancient love that is hidden inside the spirit (*rūḥ*) and the contingent love that comes from rectifying one's heart and refining one's conduct.

Let us go over these two types in detail, and to the extent that Allah opens it up to us.

The Qur'ān on Man's Ancient Love for Allah

This is the love for Allah ﷻ that is deeply embedded inside the human spirit, before each spirit was assigned a body. This is the love that emanates from the fact that this spirit is attributed to its Creator ﷻ. It is an attribution that rises above the concepts of division, connection, and separation. It transcends the measures of spatial nearness and remoteness. It suffices that its demonstrative contents are hidden and firmly established in Allah's knowledge; maybe scientific facts contained within this universe are withheld from those who are not worthy of them.

62 Translated from Imam al-Būṭī's book *Al-Ḥubb fī al-Qur'ān* (Damascus: Dār al-Fikr, 2009), 33-43.

It is that love that is indicated by and whose source is Allah's ﷻ words, His words that describe an awesome, wonderful dialogue that Allah had with the human spirit when it was a singular, comprehensive reality, and had not yet been detached from its higher realm. Rather, it was on its way towards this journey that Allah had prepared for it. Allah ﷻ says:

﴿وَإِذْ أَخَذَ رَبُّكَ مِنۢ بَنِىٓ ءَادَمَ مِن ظُهُورِهِمْ ذُرِّيَّتَهُمْ وَأَشْهَدَهُمْ عَلَىٰٓ أَنفُسِهِمْ أَلَسْتُ بِرَبِّكُمْ ۖ قَالُوا۟ بَلَىٰ ۛ شَهِدْنَآ ۛ أَن تَقُولُوا۟ يَوْمَ ٱلْقِيَـٰمَةِ إِنَّا كُنَّا عَنْ هَـٰذَا غَـٰفِلِينَ﴾

"When your Lord took out all their descendants from the loins of the children of Adam and made them testify against themselves: 'Am I not your Lord?' They said: 'We testify that indeed You are!' Lest you say on the Day of Standing: 'We knew nothing of this.'" [al-ʾAʿrāf 7:172]

Maybe you will ask: 'Where is love discussed in this verse?'

The answer is that love emanates from the hidden content of this divine address to the spirit. You should know that everything the human spirit suffers from today, such as longing and yearning, as well as any feelings of elation or sadness that take hold of it; whenever they are present, it is a remembrance of that address that its Maker ﷻ directed towards it, on a day when it had not yet been veiled inside of human bodies.

What do you think about an address that Allah directs, however He wills, towards the human spirit and the spirit then understands it and grasps it as He wills? What do you think about what this address relates, in that it was received directly by the spirit from its Maker and Creator ﷻ? What do you think about what this rhetorical question relates, this rhetorical question Allah directed towards the spirit that would then become spirits distributed in the bodies of these created slaves of Allah? What do you think about what this sweet rhetorical address relates: am I not your Lord?

It is strange that some people find this report dubious; it is a declaration that Allah ﷻ has informed us of in His Book. It is an address that He ﷻ directed towards the spirits when they were a singular, unified spirit that had not yet been divided and distributed in bodies. One of them will say: 'Here we are, however, and we are good at evoking memories. We can recall and recollect events, statements, and sounds that have been stored in our memories over the entire course of our lifetimes. We do not remember any address like the one you are talking about and describing reaching our hearing and being contained in our hearts.'

The answer is that these people are evoking their ears and looking inside a bewildering storehouse that is hidden inside their heads, searching for a memory or echoes or vibrations of that divine, ancient address. In other words, they are asking their bodies about what they might know and remember of that address. It is an astonishing question, and it is considerably foolish.

Do these people not know that it was a direct address from Allah, directly to the human spirit, without the medium of the ears or eardrums, and before there were memories that could store sounds and images in the head?

If someone then says: 'Then why do our spirits not talk to us directly about the contents of that address? Why do our spirits not give us any memory of it? Is not our only capacity to remember that which is possessed by our spirit, which is our life source? Or maybe the spirit has forgotten this address because it was so long ago, and therefore, no matter how hard we try, we will never come across anything of this address that you speak of, or that the Qur'ān talks about.'

The answer is that the spirit keeps telling you about this address and the effect that it has on it, and the longing that has overwhelmed it ever since. Do you not feel, every now and then, a yearning for something unknown? Do you not feel a longing for something that is far away from you? Do you feel a desire to humble yourself before someone, whom you look for in the latent depths of your needs and your weakness and you seek him out in everything that appears to you to be strong and capable of providing sanctuary?

All of this is nothing other than your spirit talking to you. This is how it informs you of its suffering and recalls its memories for you, and tells you about its past elation, its nights of intimacy, and when it would twitter with delight.

Let me turn your attention towards something that has escaped many of those who look for its secret and its source, which is spiritual rapture.[63] It is provoked inside you and makes you pay attention to the tunes and melodies that are recited by sweet, harmonious voices. They make you feel a mixture of yearning and longing and of joy and sadness. You do not know where they came from and where they are going.

What is the source of this rapture, which controls the spirit in those circumstances?

It is the spirit's waking up to that ancient time, the time when the divine address said: 'Am I not your Lord?' The spirit continues to long for that time, and to be affected by that address. Sorrow continues to grip it, because of its yearning for that ancient time and for that higher realm, which it was cast down from. You have not, however, found any words in any language that can translate its feelings of yearning and longing, as it is known that languages and their words are too limited and incapable of grasping the

63 I say 'spiritual rapture' (*at-ṭarb ar-rūḥī*) in order to avoid any confusion with the rhythms that stir up the soul's (*an-nafs*) impulses and arouse its animalistic and capricious desires. These have nothing whatsoever to do with the spirit, however they may vary.

feelings of the spirit. When these tunes and remedies emanating from sweet, heart-rending voices reached it, expressing something that language is incapable of translating or expressing, they touch the profundity of the feelings that dominate it, and caress everything that is stored inside of it: the yearning, the longing, and the intense memories of that ancient time. As a result, the winds of a fierce elation blow from the capacity of these tunes and melodies to express the spirit's hidden feelings, and to translate its yearning and its longing, while language – with all its rhetorical and illustrative means – cannot arrive at the blaze and agony of these feelings, and thus express them.

This is the reality of this rapture that the soul is affected by.

There are, however, people who say: 'We affirm that this rapture comes from the ability of tunes (if they emanate from sweet, harmonious voices) to arrive at the pericardium of spiritual feelings and the ability to translate them and express them. However, we do not concede that the spirit's yearning is only for what we call that ancient time. Rather, the preferred position is that it is for relationships with individuals, or forms, or places and houses. They are consolidated and from them emanate feelings of love. Maybe they will think of these things when they are away from them and long for them sleeplessly; cannot taste them as long as they are away from them, but can smell their scent. Thus, the tunes that the bearer of that soul hears are a source of rapture and elation for what it feels due to the harmony between the nature of those tunes and the sorrows that are gathered in the spirit.'

The answer is that this is the outward, which is apparent to man. It is therefore the position that is adopted by many researchers, especially those who have a materialistic worldview or a very superficial understanding of what is beyond the material.

The reality, however, is something else, and it is concealed behind the outward that we can all see. Many thinkers stop there and do not go any further.

Delving into explaining this reality requires that we provide some detail, and we seek help from Allah:

A person's spirit, whoever that person may be, feels a desire for one beloved and one beauty and no other, which is Allah. This is because the attribution between it and Allah is in effect and it is continuous, and it is absolutely out of the question that we would know how that is or how to analyse it. As for the images, shapes, and manifestations of beauty that are scattered in the vastness of this world, they are alien to it. They are extraneous to it, far removed from what it seeks and the object of its hopes.

However, what veils man from these heavenly feelings that the spirit inclines towards out of its constant yearning and longing are these animalistic impulses that Allah willed to test man with, and they continue to incline towards frivolities in the hope of satiating their desires in this worldly life, which they are dependent on.

It is from the nature of these animalistic impulses – if they do not receive adequate nurturing – to confiscate the spirit's yearning and longing towards the higher realm that it descended from, and to interpret that yearning and longing for their own benefit.

The spirit longingly yearns for the higher, eternal beauty, but the animalistic impulses within man make it focus on the fleeting beauty of this world, and they block the path that leads the spirit to the higher realm.

The spirit seeks the Uniquely Sublime, which it has known ever since that ancient time. The animalistic impulses, however, push the spirit's feelings towards their own account, and put it in front of counterfeit forms of sublimity.

The spirit looks for the Uniquely Beneficent, for whom there is no second and besides whom it knows none. Animalistic passions and impulses, however, put it in front of counterfeit forms of beneficence.

Because of what I have explained, there is, inevitably, going to be a conflict between the spirit, which inclines towards the higher realm, and the animalistic impulses, which incline towards the earthly realm.

If the animalistic impulses are not met with a constant nurturing followed by spiritual purification, these impulses will inevitably overcome the spirit in this struggle.

One of the effects of being overcome like this is that a person does not feel any of the spirit's aspirations and yearnings. Instead, he feels what his impulses dictate to him, which is their passions and desires. You thus see him taken in by images and forms and not going beyond them, imagining that they are what his spirit yearns for, when, in actual fact, the spirit is helpless and has no voice amidst the din of impulsive passions and frivolities, and earthly longings.

If a person, however, is fortunate enough to subject himself to the spiritual purification that Allah's Book calls to, and from it make it a remedy that he can be persistent with (and the foundation of this remedy is embodied in abundant remembrance of Allah and knowing that He is watching you), that is the best nourishment to strengthen the spirit, and the best way to curb the desires and passions of these impulses.

As days pass, the spirit will be invigorated by the remembrance of Allah, and the impulses' zeal will recede. Their heat will subside with time, and the spirit will eventually win a round of this struggle and thus free itself from the captivity of these animalistic impulses. This means that it will no longer be confined to counterfeit images of beauty and its various forms, which were shackling it inside the world of imaginary means and causes, which, in turn, were veiling it from seeing the causer of all causes and means.

That is when the spirit takes its bearer beyond false images of beauty and arrives at the source, at the source of beauty, at the Uniquely Beautiful, who is Allah. This is where the person can give all of his love and his true yearning and longing. That is when the spirit takes its bearer beyond the beneficence that he imagines to be coming from beneficent people and brings him to the Uniquely and Truly Beneficent, who is Allah ﷻ and gives Him alone his loyalty and exaltation.

Therefore, let us again stress that the spirit's longing is only for the higher realm that it descended from, and that its burning desire is only for that ancient time that is recorded in the memory of Allah's address to the spirits. The spirit's feelings only become confused with the din of a person's animalistic impulses and those impulses are excited, and this is because the person has not subjugated them to a constant regime of nurturing and spiritual purification.

The scholars have emphasised this reality, and have brought it back to the source that Allah's Book tells us of, summarised in the verse that we opened this second section with.[64] Someone who gave prominence to this reality is Abū ʿAlī ibn Sīnā,[65] for he illustrated the spirit's state after it had been separated from the higher realm in a poem that is demonstrative, accurate, and moving. Here is the majority of its lines:

It came down to you from an elevated place

Like doves who lived in luxury and then lost their wings

64 (tn): the second section of the first chapter of this book.
65 Abū ʿAlī Ibn Sīnā lived from 370 to 428 AH, which is 980 to 1037 CE.

Veiled from every knowing eye

It is that which showed its face and did not cover it

It arrived at you reluctantly, and maybe

It will not want to leave you, when it is in distress

It disdained and did not become familiar, and when it continued

It became familiar with being next to ruin and wasteland

I think it has forgotten times when it was in a sanctuary

And settled there, by being separated from them and not being content

It weeps when it remembers times when it was in a sanctuary,

With tear ducts that flow and have not yet run dry

Until it is almost time to go back to the sanctuary

To travel towards vaster space

It started twittering above a lofty peak

And knowledge elevates everyone who has not been elevated

Allah made it descend for a wisdom

That is hidden from the one who is sagacious, intelligent, and brilliant

This, then, is the reality of the ancient love that man has for Allah ﷻ and this is its source. Nothing can prevent man from feeling this love other than the din of his passions and the arousal of his impulses. That din is only silenced and that arousal is only subdued by what Allah the Exalted has called *at-tazkiyyah.*[66] Whoever enjoins it upon himself regularly will see the spirit's ardent love, free from the blemishes of his impulses and passions. Inevitably, he will be led, bit by bit, to the desires of his spirit, to the way of abundant remembrance of Allah and knowing that He is watching him, and to the way of constantly worshipping Him and staying away from what He has forbidden.

That is when the new, earned love, emanates from the ancient, spiritual love. Then this earned love increases with one's *tazkiyyah* and constant observance of Allah, and one attaches the blessings that come one's way to the Bestower of Blessings, may His Majesty be Manifest.

The animalistic impulses, however, remain present inside the soul, and they continue to be directed towards their desires, but they are moderate and far removed from what the spirit speaks of and aims for.

This, then, is the confirmation of what the Qurʾān says about man's ancient love for Allah.

66 (tn): i.e. spiritual purification.

Appendix C
How Do You Treat Depression?

Based on a video by Shaykh Yosri Gabr[67]

Depression is when you preoccupy yourself with worldly means and measures in order to achieve something, and when they fail, you become depressed.

Preoccupy yourself with the Creator of those means and measures and know that He is the conductor and impetus of those processes. Work with the means and measures at your disposal (to achieve your goal) and if Allah grants you success, then that is good and a blessing. If He deprives you from the result you desired, then that is good and a blessing once again because He could be depriving and stopping you from something that can cause you harm. Therefore, in both cases there is no depression. You are content and satisfied whether He grants you your desired result or not.

This was the state of Prophet Muḥammad ﷺ. For example, if the situation was that of hunger, there was a lack of food, he would intend to fast, even though if he had asked Allah to send down food from the sky, he would have been granted his request and eaten. If the disciples of ʿĪsā ibn Maryam ؑ were fed from the sky when they asked him to ask his Lord to send down a table spread with food from the sky, then surely the Prophet ﷺ would have been granted the same request.

67 https://www.youtube.com/watch?v=CjE0SEir3Ak (Accessed 29 June, 2022).

﴿إِذْ قَالَ ٱلْحَوَارِيُّونَ يَٰعِيسَى ٱبْنَ مَرْيَمَ هَلْ يَسْتَطِيعُ رَبُّكَ أَن يُنَزِّلَ
عَلَيْنَا مَآئِدَةً مِّنَ ٱلسَّمَآءِ ۖ قَالَ ٱتَّقُوا۟ ٱللَّهَ إِن كُنتُم مُّؤْمِنِينَ﴾

"And when the Disciples said, "ʿĪsā son of Maryam! Can your Lord send down a table to us out of heaven?' He said, 'Have taqwa of Allah if you are believers!'"
[al-Mā'idah 5:112]

You cannot compare the status of the Prophet ﷺ to that of the disciples of ʿĪsā. However, he did not want to eat from heaven yet, until his Ummah had eaten from it first. Therefore, he would strap a rock around his belly (to hold back his hunger) and intend to fast instead. When he was miraculously given food from his Lord during the preparation for the Battle of the Trench, when the Prophet ﷺ and the Muslim army were hungry while they were digging the trench and they had rocks tied to their bellies, he opted to feed his entire army first before himself.

Thus, we know that the Prophet ﷺ was content and satisfied in all cases and submitted his matters to Allah. Hence, he did not suffer from depression. If there was food, he was happy and if there was no food, he was happy. The case was the same with money. If he had money in his home, he would have trouble sleeping, while in your case, if you did not have money in your home on any given night, you would have trouble sleeping. You are the total opposite to the Prophet ﷺ. To be able to sleep properly, you need a full bank account, a credit card in your pocket, and you are awaiting your salary to hit your bank account, and perhaps awaiting the return of money that you loaned out to some people. Therefore, you are totally dependent on all the creations which will send sustenance your way. You are trusting in and dependent on the sustenance itself rather than depending on *ar-Razzāq*, Allah, the Provider of sustenance. However, the Prophet is reliant on *ar-Razzāq,* not on sustenance.

In one instance, the Prophet ﷺ was distributing war booty and he kept a piece of gold for a certain poor Companion who was absent and so he kept it aside for him at his own home, so that when he comes, he can give it to him. After a tiring long day as usual, the Prophet ﷺ went home to bed but on this night, he had trouble sleeping. Usually, the Prophet ﷺ, after a hard day's work, would put his head down to sleep at the end of the night and fall asleep without issue. However, that night, it was strangely different as he could not go to sleep. So, he sat up and said, 'What is wrong with me tonight?' Then he remembered the piece of gold in his house and so he got up, delivered it to the Companion and came back and slept and rested.

The Prophet ﷺ is reliant on *ar-Razzāq*, not on sustenance, *rizq*.

Do you think someone in this state can suffer from depression? He would never suffer from it his entire life.

When the Prophet ﷺ would sit in his mosque, he filled it with happiness. It would be spread everywhere and to everyone there, no one would be deprived of it. His happiness would rub off on everyone. His happiness would be dispersed to all those who felt distress and tightness in their chest and their unease would be removed as a result. Why? Because the Prophet ﷺ is with his Lord, i.e. preoccupied with and reliant on his Lord, and those who are with their Lord, truthfully and sincerely, do not suffer from depression or sadness.[68]

Question:

How does one overcome feelings of distress, heaviness and lethargy that affect your worship, such as lack of focus during reciting Qurʾān and while performing prayer?

---

68 There are people who suffer from different types of depression, such as Major Depressive Disorder, and they would be best advised to consult a mental health professional.

Answer:

Be present with people of virtue, attend congregations of *dhikr*, leave and forget your worries by being amongst good people. Associate yourself with and join good people and that will make you forget your worries. The cause of the worries in your heart is Shayṭān. He is the one that plants them in your heart and keeps making them resurface. At the same time, you might have a gloomy or moody nature that easily responds to these calls to gloom. Some people are like that, their *nafs* is melancholy. Even when they are in a state of happiness, they remind themselves of sad circumstances. They are afraid of rejoicing and being happy and they feel good being sad.

Therefore, try to avoid this glum nature or *nafs* and try to be cheerful, pleased and satisfied with Allah in both states of deprival and bestowal. Do not be of those who worship their Lord on an edge.

﴿وَمِنَ ٱلنَّاسِ مَن يَعْبُدُ ٱللَّهَ عَلَىٰ حَرْفٍ ۖ فَإِنْ أَصَابَهُۥ خَيْرٌ ٱطْمَأَنَّ بِهِۦ ۖ وَإِنْ أَصَابَتْهُ فِتْنَةٌ ٱنقَلَبَ عَلَىٰ وَجْهِهِۦ خَسِرَ ٱلدُّنْيَا وَٱلْـَٔاخِرَةَ ۚ ذَٰلِكَ هُوَ ٱلْخُسْرَانُ ٱلْمُبِينُ﴾

"Among the people there is one who worships Allah right on the edge. If good befalls him, he is content with it, but if a trial befalls him, he reverts to his former ways, losing both this world and the Next World. That is indeed sheer loss." [al-Ḥajj 22:11]

Do not worship your Lord on the condition that you are successful, your children are well, or your business is flourishing. Do not worship Allah on a condition. Worship Allah because He is Allah ﷻ. And be content with what Allah has predestined because Allah will test you with deprival and bestowal, seizing and giving, majesty and beauty. He wants to test you in every state so that you can know Him in every state.

Allah apprehends and constrains you sometimes so that you are not attached to a state of constant ease. He also facilitates and eases things for you so that you are not attached to a state of constant constraint. In doing so, you become a slave to Him alone, not a slave to the states of ease and constraint.

"He expanded you so as not to keep you in contraction; He contracted you so as not to keep you in expansion; and He took you out of both so that you do not belong to anything apart from Him." (the *Ḥikam* of Ibn ʿAṭāʾillāh al-Askandarī ﵀, number 80)

Allah does not want you to be a slave to circumstances that He established you in. He wants you to be a slave to the Creator of these circumstances.

Question:

Why are afflictions and trials intensified on the righteous people and those devoted to Allah?

Answer:

For Allah to raise their status and to make them enter Paradise from the gate of patience.

﴿إِنَّمَا يُوَفَّى ٱلصَّـٰبِرُونَ أَجْرَهُم بِغَيْرِ حِسَابٍ﴾

"The steadfast will be paid their wages in full without any reckoning." [az-Zumar 39:10]

So, when Allah wants to raise the status of a person, He afflicts him. That is why those who have had the most intense afflictions are the Prophets, the righteous, and their like. Allah also wants to wean them off this worldly life, the *Dunyā*, so that they do not get attached to it. Allah is protective over the heart of his righteous slave and does not want his heart to get attached to this worldly life and so he makes it difficult for him. Consequently, he does not enjoy it or find it beautiful and he becomes less inclined towards it. When the slave is less inclined towards this worldly life and renounces worldly pleasures, he seeks refuge in His Lord.

In doing so, Allah is also making them an example for other people. And so, when one faces a calamity of some sort, one does not think that Allah hates him because he can see that Allah treats those close and dear to Him and the Prophets in that manner and more. Therefore, Allah wants to raise him in status, and so he must be patient, convinced and content. That is why they are an example to others. Look at the lives of the Prophet ﷺ and his Companions. They are the best of this Ummah. When Allah made them live such hard lives, does that mean He hates them? Never. He made them leaders in patience and acceptance, especially the acceptance of destiny and what they were allotted in life. This is a huge form of worship.

Appendix D

Mental Illness[69]

What has Allah revealed regarding this matter and what do the authorities say?

What is the position of the Revealed Law regarding mental[70] illnesses in general and especially depression, whisperings and anxiety?

Answer (Imam Muḥammad Saʿīd Ramaḍān al-Būṭī):

To treat any illness, whether physical or psychical (*nafsī*), is permissible and preferable. However, due to the situation that we now find ourselves in, I believe that psychiatry (*at-ṭibb an-nafsī*) cannot yet be deemed successful. Rather, in most cases, its point of departure is hypotheses that are not supported by any sound science. Therefore, it is rare to see the treatment of mental illnesses produce any positive, beneficial effect. What is often imagined to be a cure is nothing more than a covering and a temporary alleviation of the illness.

69 Translated from *Maʿ an-Nās: Mashūrāt wa Fatāwa* (Damascus: Dār al-Fikr, 1423/2002), 1:184-185. The translation of this fatwa first appeared on Mahdi Lock's blog.

70 (tn): A few terms needs to be explained. The words *nafsī* translates as 'spiritual', 'mental' or 'psychical', the latter being the opposite of 'physical'. The term *ʿilm an-nafs*, literally 'the science of the *nafs*', translates as 'psychology' while *at-ṭibb an-nafsī*, or 'the medicine of the *nafs*', translates as 'psychiatry'. The major difference between a psychologist and a psychiatrist is that the latter is a medical doctor and can thus prescribe medications, while the former stays within the realm of therapy, i.e. counseling and behavioural intervention.

The secret behind this failure is that the *nafs*[71] - as scholars of the West conceive of it today, along with their students in our Muslim, Arab East - is a physical, material phenomenon. Therefore, treating any illness therein can only be – as they imagine – by going back to its presumed source, which is the body, because it is the only thing they can see in front of them.

However, the truth is that psychical phenomena in a person's life are not connected to the body and its effects, as they imagine to be the case, but rather to the spirit (*rūḥ*) and its effects. The spirit, in turn, is completely independent of the body, although it does pervade all its parts and cells just as water flows through a plant or a moist stem.

And I believe that the West is close to waking up to this fact. Today, that which is called 'science' is bringing forth a new point of view that contradicts the notion that science only moves, or indeed does not fully exist, unless it is under the sway of matter, which is everything or is the source of everything.

Thus, what is called depression or long-term mental anxiety is from the effects of the spirit, and is the consequence of some of its states. Therefore, treating illnesses like these must start from a point of view that comprises the spirit.

Since Allah ﷻ has decreed that the spirit remain one of His secrets and that its reality be beyond the knowledge of any human being, the only refuge from mental illnesses – including depression and anxiety – is to nourish the spirit with more remembrance (*dhikr*) of Allah ﷻ to turn to Him in worship and supplication, to strengthen one's faith in Allah, and to trust His wisdom and be pleased with His decision. Allah ﷻ described this treatment clearly in His Book when He said,

---

71 (tn): i.e. 'psyche' or 'soul'.

﴿أَلَا بِذِكْرِ ٱللَّهِ تَطْمَئِنُّ ٱلْقُلُوبُ﴾

"Only in the remembrance of Allah can the heart find peace." [ar-Raʿd 13:28]

In fact, true faith in Allah ﷻ is the best fortification for the soul against every evil that may lie in wait for it.

And the proof for everything we are saying is the various mental illnesses that are wreaking havoc on the western world today. Despite the best efforts of psychiatry and its practitioners, through experiments and treatments, they have failed to get rid of these illnesses.